The Blue Satin Nightgown

My French Makeover at Age 78

*To Shannon
Enjoy!
Karin Crilly*

KARIN CRILLY, MFC

The Blue Satin Nightgown: My French Makeover at Age 78

© 2016 Karin Crilly

ISBN-10: 1530473721
ISBN-13: 978-1530473724

Library of Congress Control Number: 2016904651
Published by CreateSpace

Cover Design: Fiona Jayde
Interior Design: Tamara Cribley
Author photograph: Lifetouch Portraits

Published in the United States of America

1. Memoir. 2. Self Help. 3. France

PRAISE FOR

The Blue Satin Nightgown

I loved *The Blue Satin Nightgown*. In her poignant memoir, Karin Crilly inspired me to live my dreams, no matter what. If you want to read heartfelt stories, laugh out loud, and discover recipes to nourish the body, mind, and soul, buy this book!

Leonard Szymczak, author of
The Roadmap Home: Your GPS to Inner Peace

Karin's adventures will inspire you to get started!

Dr. Hyder Zahed, author of *Create Your Legacy*

Karin writes not only about a delightful physical trip to a foreign country, but also shares the inner journey that goes with it. As a therapist, she asks the deeper questions and looks for the lessons to be learned in her own life. She manages to do this with humor and insight as well as providing an exciting travelogue and great French recipes! Enjoy! This book will fill you in many ways.

Joanne Tyson Tatham, MFC, author of *Heart Lessons*

Karin Crilly is the poster child for late-life adventures! In her late 70s and armed with a dimpled smile and a willingness to jump in to a new life, she moved to a charming small town in Southern France. She met new friends, enjoyed French food. With deep insight, Karin learns and now shares her ten poignant and deep lessons about herself, love and life. This book can help you bring more adventure, insight, and depth into your life.

Jane Myers Drew, PhD, Psychologist, author of *Where Were You When I Needed you, Dad?* and creator of the game, "Let's Connect"

There is so much of value packed tightly into this short memoir that it is difficult to begin a review simply out of fear that I will miss something vital—for so much of Karin Crilly's experience, persistence, self-actualizing enthusiasm for a life that might exhaust a less hardy soul is enthusiastically related such that it seems to demand a reader who must be at least as excited about life as she is.

But who among us could keep up so well, learn so fast, and share so deeply? Well, probably none of us—until we are nourished by the classically French recipes that feed us at the end of each chapter.

You will want to read this book at least twice, and you will definitely copy the recipes (as I did, feeling vaguely criminal, as though I were considering pilfering favorite items at a very high-end boutique along the rue du Faubourg Saint-Honoré).

Three cheers for a lady with the courage to tell the truth about herself in totally unselfconscious ways, thanks to a well-developed ability to love—her life choices, the people around her (and their antecedents), and—most certainly—herself.

Paul McNeese, Scottsdale, AZ

This book is meant to inspire readers to fulfill their dreams. In a few places, the names of some individuals and their personalities have been changed in order to protect their privacy.

This book is dedicated to my late husband, Bill. You taught me about excellence and about following my dream to live in France.

I'll be seeing you in all the old familiar places
That this heart of mine embraces all day through,
In that small café, the park across the way,
The children's carousel, the chestnut trees, the
wishing well.
I'll be seeing you in every lovely summer's day
In everything that's light and gay,
I'll always think of you that way.
I'll find you in the morning sun
And when the night is new,
I'll be looking at the moon,
But I'll be seeing you.

Written on a plaque near the Tuileries
Irving Kahal and Sammy Fain
Paris 1938

Table of Contents

Foreword

*Can we afford any half-heartedness
in the time remaining to us?*

~Roger Housden

You hold in your hands a charming memoir that explores this vital question.

Looking back from this vantage point over my own long life, I see that every one of the most meaningful events has been a result of moments of daring, being outside my comfort zone. For years, I've cultured a habit of asking myself profound questions, then awaiting the awakening they eventually bring. This one, by the poet, Mary Oliver, sparks excitement (another word for fear) in me:

> *Tell me, what is it you plan to do with your
> one wild and precious life?*

And, another by Eleanor Roosevelt:

> *What would you do if you knew you could not fail?*

No wonder my favorite books are memoirs, especially those of self-discovery, and especially this charmingly written one. Settling into my role as an armchair traveler, I embarked on a journey with an inspiring woman who had the courage and ability to play full out, trusting that serendipity and the unknown would bring rewards and greater self-knowledge. This author knew at the outset she would bank a myriad of memories she could relive in her quiet hours.

I have known Karin from a distance for years through our mutual community. But I didn't truly know her. Now, through the generosity of her sharing her late-life adventure, I have a deep appreciation for her qualities — courage, warmth and friendliness.

My own life adventures have their share of wild daring, mostly experienced within the companionship of my two husbands. I bask in partnership, and revel in the feeling that I can be quite fearless if someone has my back. So it was with eager curiosity that I read her manuscript.

Could I ever do what she did? Embark on a journey alone to a country where I don't yet speak the language, find a place to live, deal with the hassles of foreign bureaucracy, make friends? It seemed awfully risky. How does one overcome a natural tendency to shy away from such callings? It feels easier by far to seek security, safety, even while we sense such things do not actually exist.

In this inspiring story Karin has shown me that I could do as she did if I were to become fully engaged and dared greatly. If I one day find myself alone, I now sense I would have the courage to embark on such a life-affirming journey of self-discovery. I've come to trust her message that there is an alchemy that takes place when we step into the unknown, and that we will be so much richer for it.

I invite you to enjoy this enchanting true story as I did.

Read on. Trust serendipity. Expect magic.

Diana von Welanetz Wentworth *New York Times* bestselling author of ten books, including two *Chicken Soup for the Soul* titles Founder of The Inside Edge Foundation for Education (www.InsideEdge.org)

www.DianaWentworth.com

Dr. Wayne Dyer, my extraordinary muse.

Introduction

Have you ever been called to do something extraordinary? Did you act on it? How did you feel about the decision? Did the action limit or enrich your life?

Within each of us is a drive to be the best we can be. Fulfilling that desire produces an exhilarated feeling, knowing we've stretched ourselves beyond comfortable personal borders. Just as athletes strive to be better and improve their performance, so can we.

The psychologist Abraham Maslow called this invisible force self-actualization, and when reached, resulted in peak experiences. The late Wayne Dyer, renowned author and philosopher, speaks of this force as a natural, internal part of us which causes our fingernails to grow and which can't be stopped. Wayne often asked, "Have you ever tried to stop your fingernails from growing?" This force also calls us to be extraordinary.

Have you ever stopped yourself from being extraordinary?

Age does not stop this force or the desire to answer the call to be extraordinary. At age seventy-eight, I chose to ignore the familiar limiting beliefs of myself and others and expanded my life. I fulfilled a long held dream to live in France. I moved to France with a plan to stay for a year. Was the move scary? You betcha! But after living there for a year, I extended my stay for another year. And my experiences were indeed extraordinary.

Being extraordinary has always been a value of mine. During a time when women were supposed to be happy at home rearing children and caring for the house, I went back to college. I wanted my life to include more than raising a family. This act served me well after the death of my first husband, the father of my three children. Later, choosing to do what I love, I eventually became a Marriage and Family therapist and started my private practice at age forty-eight. Doing what called to me regardless of the effort, and overcoming fear — necessary to achieving my goals — led to my exceptional life.

During my thirty years as a Marriage and Family therapist, I saw my job as helping clients see their potential and believe in themselves. Once they stretched, I encouraged them to acknowledge their extraordinary effort.

Often, clients were burdened from grief, divorce, or parenting. All they wanted was relief. Yet, they wanted — no, needed me to assure them that the invisible force that wanted more from their lives was there, waiting to be uncovered. Sometimes their reluctance inspired me to share my life stories to remind them of hope. When appropriate, I revealed that my second husband had Parkinson's disease, and yet I continued to maintain a private practice while caring for him. Sharing my truth somehow encouraged clients to see their own potential.

When my husband died from complications of Parkinson's disease, I wondered if I could still be extraordinary. I had expended so much energy being his caregiver for eighteen years, the last five years of which demanded my entire being. After grieving for several years, I retired from thirty years of counseling. I needed to reinvent my life. I believed what I have always known: that the true self is presented with ideas that it is capable of fulfilling.

When I received the call at age seventy-eight, I remembered my clients and my advice to them. And I said YES!

Yes, to living a year in France, the country of my honeymoon.

Yes, to new adventures and living an extraordinary life.

Yes, to writing a book to inspire others to have dreams and live them!

My profound desire is that my story motivates you to live an extraordinary life, whatever your age! Answer that call to stretch yourself, throw off the limitations of age, and welcome the joy of your new expanded self!

You too can do something extraordinary!

The icon of Bill's favorite city

CHAPTER 1

Scattered Dreams

Nicia and I had met for lunch at Crystal Cove, a favorite spot on the California coast. The sun was shining, the air warm, as we strolled along the beach waiting for our table. Children built castles in the sand, screaming with delight as seawater washed them away.

Being cousins, we had been friends all our lives and shared secrets, joys, and pain throughout our formative, teen, adult, and now later years.

"I am thinking of taking Bill to Paris again soon," I said as we walked.

"Oh, I'm surprised."

"Well, I am scheduled to give a class in Chartres soon, so it isn't out of the question."

My husband Bill had spent his entire career in the airline industry. He traveled all over the world with his work and Paris was his favorite place to return to.

"I am hoping you might join us, Nicia," I continued.

Nicia jerked slightly at the unexpected invitation but said she would give it some thought.

We were summoned to lunch. We turned from our stroll and headed back to the waiting table.

By the time we arrived, Nicia had made up her mind. "I'd love to join you and Bill."

In Paris, Nicia and I put our heads together as we sat in the elegant lounge at the Plaza Athénée enjoying a glass of Pinot Grigio. We had a plan to carry out. The hotel was as familiar to me now as when Bill and I spent the first week of our honeymoon here thirty years ago.

I recalled how Bill, with his love of excellence and detail, had literally spent weeks planning our seventeen-day trip from Paris to the Cote d'Azur. Because we both loved fine dining, the restaurants we stopped at during our drive along the gourmet trail had to be Michelin-starred.

After another sip of wine, I spied some unusual potted plants on a nearby table. Nodding my head as if to say, "This is the spot," I brought out the wooden box with Bill's ashes.

I looked around the lounge, decorated in gold and white with Louis XV chairs. Spectacular chandeliers illuminated the room, but we were alone, the perfect opportunity, I took the small bag with Bill's ashes out of the box. Taking a deep breath, I donated some of the powdery flakes to the soil in the pot.

"I'm curious what you were thinking and feeling as you sprinkled those ashes," said Nicia.

With a heavy heart, I said, "I recalled how Bill whispered wistfully several times during that last year of his life, 'I want just one more trip to Paris.' Knowing he was too frail for the journey, I had to say no. It was so painful to deny that generous man anything. Now I am satisfying his last wish."

Nicia looked at me with admiration. "I'm so glad you asked me to join you. This mission would have been difficult by yourself."

"Shall we head for scene number two?" I asked, wanting to leave this location so full of memories.

Not far away was the second place I had chosen. We walked the short distance to Pont Neuf, a bridge over the Seine where it is possible to get to a walkway along the river Seine.

How many evenings had ended with a walk along the Seine? We were so in love with Paris and each other that we didn't want the evening to end. I always felt like we were Gene Kelly and Leslie Caron in *An American in Paris*, dancing along the *quai*.

When we reached the Pont Neuf, I stood with Nicia and thanked Bill for those memories as the slow-moving waterway accepted my lover, my friend, my soulmate.

Our third destination was the Eiffel Tower, another of Bill's favorite restaurant spots. We took the *Métro* and soon ascended at the Tour Eiffel stop. The iconic Tower loomed above as Nicia and I found an inconspicuous bench at one corner of the park where the grass was a vibrant green. Like the former two places, we were serene and reflective until the right moment became clear.

Families and couples strolled by and an ice cream vendor pushed his cart. The vendor, with his snacks, reminded me of the time Bill accompanied me on a school field trip. I told Nicia the story. "I took my class on an outing with a forest ranger to demonstrate the life cycle of a silk worm. As the lecture got lengthier, the students became restless, Bill felt sorry for them so started handing out the snacks we'd brought along. As the students noticed, one by one they went to Bill for a treat, causing the ranger to end the lesson."

"That sounds just like Bill, always thinking of making others happy," Nicia replied.

With that, I was ready to give the green grass a little extra nourishment and another mental hug to the man who brought joy to so many. I wiped the tears flowing down my cheeks.

Nicia and I now made our way to Île Saint-Louis for the last stop on our pilgrimage The emotions of the day had been heavy, so I was ready to lighten the mood here, a place so important to Bill he would never leave Paris without paying his respects. Bill loved ice cream and indulged in many helpings of the famous Berthillon *glace*.

"I see Bill isn't the only one to enjoy Berthillon's. There's a line of people waiting," Nicia remarked.

Leaving a part of Bill wasn't so easy this time; the one door open to the sidewalk was filled with customers. Finally our opportunity came. Nicia held the door ajar while I poured flakes onto the sidewalk side of the door. Now he too was in line!

Together we thought: *Sorry, Bill, for not finding a more permanent spot*. In life, ice cream melted too quickly, just as our life together had ended too quickly.

Scattering Bill's ashes in Paris changed something in me. I was saying goodbye to the past, readying myself for a new life. Oh, how I loved Bill and would forever miss him. But at seventy-eight, I was about to embark on the biggest adventure of my life as I moved to the city of my dreams, Aix-en-Provence.

A fountain and plane trees on Cours Mirabeau

CHAPTER 2

New Beginnings

She Believed She Could, So She Did

How does one move to France at age seventy-eight after the death of a husband?

Here's what I did:

Two necessary projects loomed the largest before I could move. The first was to obtain a Long Stay Visa for France and the other was preparing my house for prospective tenants to lease during the time I would be out of the country. I knew there would be monumental tasks, so I prepared my list with steps to follow to fulfill a dream and have an adventure.

1. Prepare Mentally and Emotionally

My passion for my adventure propelled me forward. Some people become paralyzed by fear. Not me! I was so focused on the excitement of discovery in the year ahead, I had no anxiety-ridden thoughts. Those would come later.

2. Face and Overcome Obstacles

I needed to tackle the bureaucracy to obtain a Long Stay Visa. I had to make an appointment to appear in person at the French Consulate and bring the following documents:

a. Current passport valid for six months after my return
b. Proof of Residency
c. Clean record from local police department (thank goodness I wasn't caught smoking dope when I was young).
d. A letter declaring non-employment during my stay
e. A statement declaring the purpose of my visit
f. Financial statements showing I could support myself for the year
g. Medical insurance for the year
h. Two passport-type color photos
i. Express Mail self-addressed envelope

At the time of the appointment, I had to fill in a form written in French. Really? I brought along a French-speaking friend to help me. I also needed to pay a processing fee. I allowed plenty of time for this process, at least six weeks before my departure date, but not before three months prior to my leave.

Whew! Who said dreams come easily?

3. Eliminate Baggage to Realize a Dream

Now to the second project. I first hoped to rent my house furnished to minimize the amount of work for me to get it ready. But most tenants wanted it unfurnished, so I began the monumental task of divesting my belongings from a home I had lived in for seventeen years.

How does one begin? I started from the premise that I wanted to get the smallest storage space available. Every item in my house needed to be screened and categorized: take, store, sell, give away, or throw away. The overwhelming task required the help of family and friends to keep me focused. One friend evaluated my clothes by asking me if it was one of my favorites, checking its condition and whether it was multi-purpose. Anything glitzy didn't make the cut for a French wardrobe. She also helped determine if I would take it with me or have Vicki, my daughter, mail it to me later. My son-in-law John assessed electronic equipment. Vicki knew what furniture and artwork I valued enough to want to pay storage. I sold large items on Craigslist, donated my art easel and art supplies to a local art college, and gave the rest to the Salvation Army.

When it came to Bill's belongings, I wasn't ready for that emotional journey yet. I boxed and stored them.

I took three months to complete my household project. At the end of each day, I plopped exhausted into bed. Even though I was highly motivated and eager to start my new adventure, the process was emotionally draining.

4. Plan Ahead

It was important to have my temporary home away from home arranged in advance. I had searched for my hotel on the Internet in the area I preferred. I had a friend in Cannes look at the place for me before I arrived. I booked the hotel for the one week it would take to find an apartment. Thank goodness for friends! That takes me to the next item.

5. Surround Yourself With Supportive People

I had the support of my family and friends who frequently told me how adventurous I was. My two daughters, Wendy and Vicki, were so proud of me, they told all of their friends. Vicki actually went with me to France for three weeks to be part of my new life.

During my three-month preparation period, only one person suggested I might be lonely or might want to come home early.

6. Say Goodbye

Now, I had really done it! All the planning, the divesting of my personal belongings in order to make my house ready for the tenants, and getting the French Long Stay Visa were accomplished. I said good-bye for now to family and friends through a beautiful party given to me by Wendy and Vicki at the gracious home of Dick and Mary Schiendler. All of the preparations were behind me and I was ready for what awaited. I felt triumphant for my accomplishment and eager to begin my new adventure!

7. Say Hello to Adventure!

October 2012, three months after initiating my project, the sun was shining brightly as the taxi turned down the boulevard Cours Mirabeau, the main street in Aix-en-Provence I had dreamed about but hadn't seen for thirty years. It was just as I remembered: doublewide sidewalks with mature plane trees, those sycamore-like trees with five-fingered leaves, marching the length of the avenue, stretching up like lovers reaching for each other in an embrace of foliage.

"I'm really here!" I told my daughter Vicki. "My skin is covered in goose bumps."

"Mine is too. I love the old buildings. They are not anything like we have in California," Vicki responded.

"They are eighteenth-century homes, but were later turned into apartments and businesses."

"And look at all of the outdoor cafés along the street," exclaimed Vicki who loved the ambience of the French people sitting and chatting.

In my mind, Bill was there, too. How complete this would be if he were here with me. It hit me again, as it would many times, that I'd committed to living here for a year by myself.

The taxi stopped in front of the Grand Hotel Negre Coste, my new home for a week until I found an apartment. The driver unloaded my three large suitcases containing all of my possessions for the coming year, and Vicki's one suitcase, which contained all she needed for her three weeks in France. The hotel desk clerk ran out to help carry in the bags filled with my laptop, a few pictures, and clothes. I took one more look around my beloved Cours Mirabeau to drink in the serenity of an October day in Aix. With a deep breath, I walked into the hotel to discover my temporary living quarters.

Settled into my room, I began unpacking enough for the week. As I took out a pair of walking shoes, I flashed back eighteen years when I first realized something was not right with Bill. We were walking near our house in Laguna Beach.

As we strolled, I said, "Bill, are you aware your left arm is not moving as you walk, and you're dragging your left foot?"

He was silent for a few minutes, then said, "No, I'm not feeling that." We both agreed that he needed to see a doctor to check if he'd had a stroke.

At the appointment, our doctor gave his diagnosis: Parkinson's disease. It took some time to let the ramifications of what that meant sink in. Two high achievers, naive about the nature of this disease, we wouldn't let circumstances stand in our way. We were certain we could beat this too, with right action and positive thinking. Little did we know what lay ahead.

Holding one shoe in my hand, I snapped back to unpack my suitcase. Through the open window, I heard the sound of birds outside the hotel.

Vicki looked out the window. "They must be swallows, Mom," she said.

The sudden swarming flights and squawking of Provence's swallows would keep me company in the days and weeks to come as they woke me up each morning.

Vicki helped put away some of my things, and then became restless. "Let's get out and explore the city."

Vicki and I had traveled together before, spending a month in Mexico some years back. I knew how adept she was at navigating new surroundings, picking up a foreign language, and adapting to a new culture. She was the perfect person to help me get settled and to deal with the many intricacies of my new surroundings.

"Great idea. We'll have time later to unpack. Let's look for the *agent immobilier* I've been emailing, who sent me pictures of apartments."

The realtor's office was close by in an eighteenth-century limestone building with pillars on the front. The interior was decorated in a modern glass and steel style. I soon learned that this mix of modernity with the ancient was not unusual in Aix.

Entering the office, I spoke in English and asked for François.

"He is not in this office," the receptionist informed us. "He works in another town."

How strange, I thought, because he gave this location as his address. I asked if someone else could show us the property with the reference number 2483, the one that seemed perfect for me. I found out that only the listing agent could show his properties, so was told to come back the next day when he should be in the office.

With great anticipation, Vicki and I returned the next day only to find François absent again. We chose another agent. I told her that since I had no car and would need to walk everywhere, I wanted to be in the centre ville. She listened carefully and then proceeded to tell us she had the perfect place for me slightly out of town, a good match for a single woman.

"The walk to town would be so good for your health," she said, with a big smile.

"That won't work for me. Surely you have other apartments."

"No, I really don't," she said.

I explained how in America we have a system where every apartment in the area is available for any agent to show.

"In France, each agent has his or her listings and can only show those listings," she explained.

"So for me to see every apartment available to rent in Aix, I have to go to every *immobilier* in town?"

"Yes, that is true. That is how it works, and I have only the one place to show you."

It seemed unbelievable, but what could I do but go with their system? Vicki and I then agreed to see her property.

The apartment was on the grounds of a beautiful old villa, with lots of trees and a sculptured fountain in the center of a manicured green lawn. Unfortunately, the flat itself was not attractive; plus, I couldn't see myself either living there or walking the one kilometer uphill in the rain with groceries to get home. I told that to Sabine, but all the way down the hill to her office, she continued to tell me all the good things about living there.

Vicki and I found another office close to the hotel and paid Florence, a new property agent, a visit. Her office was in a seventeenth-century building in the oldest part of Aix, the Mazarin area. After ringing the bell, she buzzed us in and we climbed our way up some very old stone steps to the *premiere étage* (first floor, which was actually the second floor). Again, we were delighted to find ourselves in a modern office decorated with museum-like sculptures from Paris.

I told her what I was looking for, to which she replied she didn't have anything, as she dealt mostly with sales. We chatted a bit, then she suddenly said, "But wait, my husband has a friend with an apartment that might be available."

She called him, and sure enough it would be available in three weeks. We made an arrangement to see it the next day.

The apartment was an easy walk from her office, though I wondered why she walked us in a roundabout way. I would find out why later. Salespeople are the same the world over.

The apartment turned out to be a beautifully appointed flat. I was immediately charmed by the high ceilings, the sculptured ornamentation on the walls, and the faux fireplace. Decorated in gray and purple, it had an open kitchen, which I liked, and two bedrooms, perfect for the many visitors I anticipated. There was a bathroom fit for a queen, with walls covered in metallic tile and the largest egg-shaped bathtub I've ever seen. It was in the *centre ville*. I was sold.

The next steps would have been daunting had I not had Vicki supporting and encouraging me along the way. First, I needed a French bank account and tenant's insurance before being able to rent. No problem, I thought. This was when I learned the French work ethic differed from that of the American. The French person enjoys a thirty-five hour workweek with six weeks of annual paid vacation. Work definitely doesn't own the soul of a French person.

I entered a bank close to Florence's office, intent on procuring the necessary documents. A young man, seated close to the front door, said, *"Bonjour, puis-je vous aider?"* (Good day, could I help you?)

I told him my business in English; he immediately switched to my language. Soon I began to understand that in France, administrative tasks were carried out in slow motion. One didn't just walk into a bank and open an account. No, one made an appointment. Since it was Friday, I hoped to finish my business by the end of the day.

Pierre—as I learned his name was—frowned. "It's the end of the French workweek. I can make an appointment for you to come back on Monday to open an account."

I shrugged my shoulders and he continued. "You will need several documents to open an account. Be sure to bring your passport and your *visa de long séjour.*"

I looked perplexed at Vicki, as he explained, "Long Stay Visa and proof of address." I took this to mean the hotel where I was staying and later learned of a surprise.

"They will request you to give your signature, and in return will give you a debit card and tell you the monthly administration fee."

"Thank you," I replied, With that, he wrote the appointed time on a card and handed it to me.

As I was about to leave, I noticed he hadn't written my time in a book, so I asked if he needed to jot it down. Was he rushing to enjoy the weekend?

"Oh, I'll remember *you.*"

I walked away from the bank, pondering. What was that all about?

How ironic that just one month ago upon retiring, I felt a loss of identity. And now here was someone in a foreign country who would remember me? A seventy-eight-year-old retired Marriage and Family Therapist reinventing herself was going to be recognized? I secretly hoped he was making a pass at me.

On Monday, the bank receptionist Pierre did indeed remember me, and he showed me into an office where I met the bank manager to open my account. He told me that my hotel address wasn't good enough. I needed a permanent address in France to open a bank account. Huh? I couldn't rent a home without a bank account, and I couldn't have a bank account without a place to live! Thank goodness for my Vicki. She put the problem back into their lap.

"My mother needs to have a bank account in order to rent an apartment. What can she do?"

We sat and waited as he rubbed his chin thoughtfully.

"Hmm, there might be another way." He told Vicki I could buy tenant's insurance, which will enable me to open an account.

Two hours later, I was the proud owner of a French bank account and tenant's insurance for an apartment I didn't have! Slightly frustrated with the system, yet again triumphant, I took the bank and insurance papers to Florence's office, where she had prepared the many contracts to be signed.

As I reached for my checkbook to write checks for my new apartment and for Florence, I sensed Bill again.

He was supposed to be here with me. Thirty years ago, we'd vowed to be back in France together. So why was I here by myself?

I was again reminded that one of the hardest things about losing a spouse was recognizing that person was no longer present and sharing my life. I had to face each new day alone. The thrill I was feeling only a moment before had disappeared. Sadness had crept into the idea of being here solo.

Florence interrupted my thoughts. "You can now boast of having a French apartment."

Her enthusiasm was contagious and my joy returned. "Yes, and it is in the *centre ville!*"

Unfortunately, Vicki's three weeks in France were up before my move into the apartment. But at least she was with me when I first saw the flat and gave it her hearty approval.

"Mom, I see my flight for home leaves at 8 a.m. from Marseilles airport," Vicki said.

"That means leaving Aix-en-Provence at 5 a.m. on the bus to the airport. I'll walk with you to the station; I don't want you walking alone in the dark with a roll-on suitcase and a carry-on bag," I said.

"Mom, I'll be fine, I don't want you to be out that early and that would mean you walking home in the dark alone."

"We seem to be at a stand-off. I'll order a taxi just to relieve my concern," I replied.

"That works for me."

Out in the street before daylight watching for the taxi, mother and daughter shared a tearful good-bye, the younger sad to be leaving her senior alone in a country far, far away without support, the older trying to reassure her that all would be well, even if not fully believing it herself. The taxi arrived on time, suspending a prolonged emotional good-bye.

The suitcases were stowed, the destination given and my constant partner of the last three weeks sped off in the dark of night. For the first time, I was alone in this adventure of mine. Fear and excitement raced through my veins.

Move-in Day

As promised, Florence showed up to help me — three hours after the appointed time. "Oh, Carine, I am so sorry, I got held up in a meeting. But I am here now and we need to load quickly so we don't hold up the traffic!"

I was not surprised to see her with an Audi convertible parked outside. Realtors in California drive high-end cars and I figured it would be the same here. I was a little shocked to see one side dented as though she'd scraped it while driving through the narrow one-way streets of the Mazarin. We quickly stowed my three large suitcases in her car while the traffic lined up behind us, waiting like captives eager to see us move on. I fastened my seatbelt and off I went, transported by Florence driving like a maniac.

Odeon, tall, thin, handsome, and my new landlord, was waiting for us at my new abode, on Rue Emeric David. He helped lift the suitcases up to the *première étage* while Florence sped off. Did she have another meeting?

Or was she concerned I would discover too soon what would cause me to move within a few months?

The first Friday night in my apartment, I felt the floor rattle. *Ba Boom. Ba Boom. Ba Boom.* Florence didn't tell me my beautiful new surroundings were located over a nightclub that played disco music every Friday and Saturday nights until 2 a.m.! With my bedroom located directly over the club, I held onto my bed as the pulsating beat rattled the floor. *Ba Boom Ba Boom!* I had to wait until closing time to settle my nerves and get some sleep.

France did not have disclosure laws when it came to renting apartments. I wondered what else I would learn about my new home in France.

I loved discovering my new environment, Aix-en-Provence. My greatest joy was walking the streets luxuriating in viewing the seventeenth- and eighteenth-century architecture of the buildings. Nothing in my native Southern California rivaled what I saw. I became familiar with my new home and learned the locations of the one hundred fountains for which the small city was famous.

My walks were filled with photo opportunities of interesting gateways; my favorite fountain, the *quatre* dolphins in the Mazarin Quarter; an old-fashioned baby perambulator in front of an antique store with ivy growing artfully along one wall. Tall imposing walls came right up to the sidewalk, with the occasional open gate revealing an interesting courtyard within. It was obvious some doorways were openings for a carriage entrance, now too small and awkward for an automobile. The houses I most enjoyed had high walls with iron gates where I could see within, whether they were open or not.

Cours Mirabeau, the main street originally laid out in 1651 and once used as a road for horse-drawn carriages, was my favorite street in all of Aix. Its doublewide sidewalks on both sides of the street are lined with plane trees, which are similar to sycamore trees with heavy spotted trunks. Their branches spread out, providing shade from the brutal Provençal sun. The road began with the impressive *Rotonde*, a large fountain which formed a roundabout built in 1859 to mark the entrance of the city when coming from Marseilles. The center of the fountain held three maidens standing on a platform representing Justice, Agriculture, and the Beaux Arts, the virtues of Aix-en-Provence. Cherubs riding water-spewing swans formed the lower fountain. At the other end of the street was a statue of *Roi Rene*, one of Aix's most influential and beloved rulers. A one-hundred-year-old traditional treat, the *calisson*, a cookie, was said to have been made for King Rene in honor of his second wife, and its diamond shape represented her delicate lips.

I became familiar with the stores and restaurants in the *centre ville*. I spied a crêpe stand, and ordered one to be filled with Grand Marnier.

I flashed back to when I first met Bill in California in 1981, an energetic, well-toned man with black hair streaked with white and sparkling brown eyes. I noticed him standing out from the crowd as he was serving crêpes at a homeowners' brunch. I later learned he had made sixty-seven of them earlier. He heated and served them with a choice of four different fillings, two savory and two sweet. I watched this efficient man take orders and fill the crêpes as requested, serving the plate to the partygoer. No woman hovered over or helped him. A single woman, I decided to go over to talk to him. I told him I was a newcomer to the area and happy to be invited to the brunch. I sat down to eat my delicious crêpe filled with Grand Marnier, and Bill came over to talk with me when he had a break. We discovered we both played tennis and made a date to play the next day. That was the beginning of a fast-paced romance leading to our marriage and *lune de miel Française* (French Honeymoon). Even our romance began over French food.

The French crêpe I ordered was tasty, but not as delectable as Bill's.

As I strolled the city, I started observing the women and what it was that made them look so distinctive. First of all, a Frenchwoman didn't leave her house without being fully put together with matching scarf, shoes, and handbag. She usually had a great haircut, even though it wasn't always coiffed to perfection. And I didn't meet a Frenchwoman without perfect posture. No matter the age, she didn't stoop. Even the babies and little girls were dressed in complete ensembles. Everything matched. I learned that being well dressed was about being respectful and not insulting the people she would meet. No wonder women were so well groomed. They started as babies being conscious of how to dress before going outside.

I, too, learned to give up my California casual dress soon after my arrival. Even though it was fall weather, and the temperature was still in the upper eighties, women always completed an outfit with a matching scarf. I remembered buying several for my wardrobe, tying each carefully before leaving my apartment. After half an hour in the warm Provençal sun, I was perspiring so badly, my neckerchief came flying off! I still didn't know how the Frenchwomen tolerated them in the heat. But at least the rest of me was color-coordinated, and as the weather began to cool, I was well stocked with the mandatory scarf. The other part of my dress that I quickly learned was inappropriate were my white sneakers. They were a sure sign of a tourist. After all, I was now a French woman.

One day while enjoying lunch at a popular sidewalk café, Les Deux Garçons, I noticed a couple at the next table watching me.

"Do you live here? We are wondering where the Granet Museum is located," the female said.

"I live here now. I just moved from California."

"Really! What brought you to Aix?" she asked.

This question often arose as I talked to people at the cafés. In the beginning, I always answered the same way. "I fell in love with Aix thirty years ago when I was here on my honeymoon. I always knew I would be back." But as time went on, I reconsidered the question. What caused me to leave everything familiar, including family and friends, to come to a place where I knew no one?

Over time, my heart revealed a quest. I came to France looking for adventure. I wanted a place where everything was new and exciting. Each day, I was transported out of the ordinary into the excitement of discovery in this foreign land.

I also began to realize I have never wanted to live an unremarkable life, which at this stage of my life often meant staying planted where I lived, doing what I had always done. I had lived in Southern California most of my life, and was very familiar with the geography, the customs, the happenings, the weather, and the people. I could have stayed where all was comfortable and known, but with my appetite for excitement, I still had the desire to investigate other cultures of the world and continue to learn my entire life.

My move to Aix-en-Provence posed two questions:

1. "Could I, who survived the grief of my husband's death, move to a foreign country, let go of the past and carve out a life by myself?"
2. "What would bring meaning and fulfillment to this stage of my life?"

My life was not over, but just beginning again in a foreign country.

Crêpes Suzette

Crêpes

Ingredients:

2 large eggs

3/4 cup all-purpose flour

1/2 cup milk

1/8 teaspoon salt

1/2 teaspoon sugar

1/3 cup cold water

1 tablespoon canola oil

1 tablespoon melted unsalted butter, plus more butter for the skillet

In a medium bowl, whisk together the eggs, flour, milk, salt and sugar until smooth, the batter will be thick. Whisk in the water, oil, and melted butter.

Heat a 6-inch crêpe pan or nonstick skillet and rub with a little butter. Add 2 tablespoons of the batter and tilt the skillet to distribute the batter evenly, pouring any excess batter back into the bowl. Cook over moderately high heat until the edges of the crêpe curl up and start to brown, about 45 seconds. Flip the crêpe over and cook for 10 seconds longer, until a few brown spots appear on the bottom.

Tap the crêpe out onto a baking sheet.

Repeat with the remaining batter to make 12 crêpes, buttering the skillet a few times as necessary.

Orange Butter

Ingredients:

6 tablespoons unsalted butter, softened, plus more for buttering

1/4 cup plus 2 tablespoons sugar, plus more for sprinkling

2 tablespoons cognac

1/4 cup Grand Marnier

1 tablespoon finely grated orange zest

1/3 cup fresh orange juice

In a mini food processor, blend the 6 tablespoons of butter with 1/4 cup of the sugar and the orange zest. With the machine on, gradually add the orange juice until incorporated.

Preheat the broiler. Butter a large rimmed baking sheet and sprinkle lightly with sugar. Place a crêpe, flat, on the baking sheet. Place 2 rounded teaspoons of the orange butter in the center of each crêpe. Fold the crêpe in half, and in half again to form triangles; arrange on the prepared baking sheet, pointing them in the same direction, and overlapping slightly. Sprinkle with the remaining 2 tablespoons of sugar and broil on the middle shelf of the oven until they begin to caramelize, about 2 minutes.

Using a long spatula, transfer the crêpes to a heatproof platter.

Meanwhile, in a small saucepan, heat the Grand Marnier and cognac. Ignite carefully with a long match and pour the flaming mixture over the crêpes. Tilt the platter and, with a spoon, carefully baste the crêpes until the flames subside. Serve right away.

CHAPTER 3

Vignettes of Street Life in Aix

If you are lucky enough to have lived in Paris as a young man, then wherever you go for the rest of your life it stays with you, for Paris is a moveable feast.

Ernest Hemingway

I settled in my own apartment in the *centre ville* of Aix-en-Provence and I learned how to cook on an electric stove (I'd always preferred gas). I couldn't quite master the combination washer/dryer that took three hours to complete its cycle, only to have damp clothes that still needed hanging. I purchased three jasmine plants and a trellis, and coerced the plant man to deliver them. I discovered that Monoprix, the local grocery store, would deliver my shopping if I spent fifty euros — easy to do with a few bottles of wine.

I think Florence, my realtor, felt guilty because she phoned the next week.

"*Bonjour*, Carine," she announced on the phone. It is Tuesday, *marché*, market day. All of the French buy their produce at the *marché*. Have you been out to shop?"

"No, but I'd like to talk about the apartment."

"Oh, I don't have time to talk, now. I'm off to another meeting. So nice to chat with you. Go to the *marché*. *Bonjour*." Florence left me no time to complain about the disco under my bedroom.

I looked out the window and saw that the parking lot had been converted into a sea of colorful stalls. I jumped at the prospect of a new adventure. Indeed, the market was a madhouse of activity and tables with seasonal produce, cheeses, spices, baked goods, meat, fish, and rotisserie chickens.

Initially, I was overwhelmed by the excitement, but soon entered in like a local. I crowded in with the other people and checked out each stall for the freshest produce brought in from the countryside. Everywhere anticipation was in the air. One vendor/farmer provided me with a plastic basket to place my vegetables. He would then separate and weigh each item, then give me the price. I paid the euros, and he handed me my purchase. In a resounding voice, he said, "*Merci, au revoir, Madame.*"

Before I could say, "*Merci,*" another customer moved in with her basket.

Most French shoppers at the market didn't drive to the market. Sometimes they walked long distances or came by bus. They placed their purchases into a *chariot* or basket on wheels. It was more sensible than carrying heavy bags, which was not good for posture. The French did not stoop!

I got caught up in all the fragrances and the hustle and bustle of the people pushing and crowding. But I quickly became overwhelmed, not because I wasn't used to shopping or planning a meal, but because of the interaction and variety of products being offered. Every purchase required a human interaction and exchange of energy. I could feel a pulse and vibrancy between people that was not present in the modern supermarket experience.

As the weeks went by, I learned to make a list before venturing out into the very hectic *marché* scene, but always would end up improvising, based on the new seasonal choices. I made the rounds of the vendors with confidence before settling on the stall that had the fruit and vegetables to my liking. I participated in the obligatory greeting of *"Bonjour,"* picked up the plastic basket to hold my choices, filled it with what I wanted, and handed it to the vendor, and paid the euros and stowed the purchases in my French *chariot* as I repeated, *"Merci, au revoir,"* just like the locals.

I loved to check out the fresh fish stall. The aroma transported me to Saturday mornings in San Francisco. Bill and I shared a weekly ritual of visiting our favorite specialty stores to buy the freshest items for our weekend meals. First to North Beach to Molinari's Italian Deli, then on to Stella's Bakery for the longest and tastiest bread sticks to accompany my specialty, a San Francisco recipe for Red Butter. We always took in the Farmers Market at the Marina, which determined what seasonal vegetables would appear on our menu. The fish market in Sausalito was the last stop for the fresh catch of the day, arriving just as the fishermen returned to the dock. Shopping complete, we would rush home to prepare our weekend meals together. Bill was a gourmet cook and one of his greatest joys was to be involved in meal planning and preparation.

Lost in my reverie at the *marché*, I thought how Bill would have loved it here. He enjoyed flowers, so I headed to my favorite flower *marché* held in the Place de l'Hôtel de Ville, which was actually the government building fashioned after an Italian palace. It became my favorite spot, not only for the fresh flowers and plants which I loved, but because it was in one of the most beautiful and historic settings in Aix. A great plaza to drink coffee and admire the beautiful surroundings! Locating a perfect spot to sit in the outdoor café under a plane tree, I would signal the waiter. *"Un café, s'il vous plait."*

As I sipped my coffee, I would people watch and enjoy the picturesque spot with stalls of local, seasonal flowers in vivid colors. After my coffee, I shopped for flowers for my apartment. The big, round beautiful peonies reminded me of doll heads; I admired the many varieties of roses and gladiolas in multiple shades and sizes. The French, like me, loved flowers. As a result, the market thrived as shoppers made their choices among the new blooms.

When I handed the vendor flowers, he asked, "Is this for you or a gift?"

Either response received a carefully wrapped joy to carry home. The French took great pride in wrapping and presenting their products. This reminded me of another event from the past.

A large part of my life with Bill involved traveling — a passion for both of us. During one of our trips, Bill and I were walking in Paris. We wanted a little munchie to tide us over until *déjeuner,* so we wandered into a patisserie. Picking out an item for each of us, the clerk began wrapping them. In our limited French, we tried to indicate we just needed them in a napkin in order to eat as we walked. Evidently we didn't communicate well, because she proceeded to put them together and took the time to carefully make a box out of the decorated paper and tied it up with a ribbon!

Like the French, Bill and I took pride in our endeavors. From finding the freshest ingredients to cooking them precisely, to eating with gusto, we cherished our time together around food.

As the weeks passed by, I realized I was having the adventure of my life. So many things were happening that I could not have imagined in my native country. I became more alive observing everything new around me.

On the way home from a gourmet lunch with new friends held at Pierre Reboul, a starred Michelin restaurant, I was approached by a young Frenchman. He said something to me in French.

"Parlez-vous Anglais?" I said.

"I like the way you are dressed," replied a thirty-something year old man with sandy red hair and a neatly trimmed beard. His blue eyes kept veering toward my legs, as if there was a magnetic pull.

"*Merci*," I said, thanking him. I told him about the luncheon at Pierre Reboul. "Do you know that restaurant?"

"No, but I really like the way you are dressed, especially your stockings. They are stockings, aren't they?"

I looked down at the stockings I had bought at Eurodif, a store I usually referred to as the J.C. Penney's of France. They had black seams up the back. I hadn't seen those in a long time, but figured it must've been a French thing.

Somewhat nervous, I quickly changed the subject and asked if he lived in Aix.

"Yes, I live in Aix and work as a journalist."

"Oh. What paper or magazine?"

"Not any one in particular," he said as he continued looking at my legs. "I really like your stockings. May I see them?"

I thought, *You* are *seeing them!* Clearly, he had something else on his mind and it wasn't stockings!

"Thank you for your interest, but I am old enough to be your grandmother!"

"Oh, I don't mind that." He winked. "Are you sure you don't have time to show me your stockings?"

I muttered, "Put a sock in it," and quickly walked the half block to my home. When I was close to my front door, I turned to see if he had disappeared. He was still standing, watching my stockings. My hose and I walked past my door, in case he was a stocking stalker.

Street view in the Mazarin

Oh how I loved this country! At seventy-eight years old, I'd found a place in the world where I was noticed. What a revelation!

On another day, I walked home from grocery shopping with a bag of vegetables. A twelve-year-old boy rode his bicycle while his two companions, a girl and a boy, walked beside him.

The boy stopped his bicycle beside me and asked in French, *"Qu'est-ce que c'est?"* (What are those?)

I replied with my customary, *"Parlez-vous Anglais?"*

He pointed to the green leaves sticking out of my shopping bag, and asked in English, "What is that?"

"Celery."

"May I see?"

I wondered if this was a distraction so his friends could take my wallet. I kept an eye on them while I pulled the whole stalk out of my sack.

"What do you call that in English?"

Again, I said, "Celery."

He repeated the word several times in English to his friends. They nodded and repeated, "C-e-l-e-r-y," to memorize it.

Did he think it was marijuana or some other exotic plant? A French friend later told me the answer. In France, it was common to sell celery by the individual rib. The boy may have wondered what all the leaves were.

He then sped off into the crowd with his friends. The boy's curiosity spurred my own wonderment. He didn't see me as a foreigner who he should avoid talking to, but merely another member of the community who had something of interest. He made me feel at home in my new surroundings.

The innocence of this interaction made me realize how easy it was to be fearful and on guard in a new culture. Maintaining a sense of curiosity opened new doors. I vowed to keep my doors open — except to stocking stalkers.

Many people in the United States mistakenly believed that people living in France were rude to visitors. I have often been asked how I tolerated their arrogance. However, in my time there, I experienced the very opposite. On the *Métro* when I was traveling with clearly too much luggage, businessmen who appeared in a hurry to get to their offices often paused to help me up or down the stairs. I always told them their mother would be proud of them!

After I had been in Aix for several months, a little note came from *La Poste* to pick up a box of clothing sent by my daughter. When I arrived, I found the box too large and heavy to carry back to my apartment. I inquired about a taxi, but there was none. I must have looked discouraged, because one of the postal clerks came out from behind the counter and showed me to a bench outside. If I could wait fifteen minutes, she would be finished with her work for the day and would drive my package and me home.

Delighted, I sat in the designated spot and enjoyed the afternoon sun, thinking of her graciousness. At the appointed time, out she came carrying my box. She indicated that I follow her to her Fiat in the parking lot across the street. She loaded the box into the back seat of her little car and off we went.

She drove me home, parked her Fiat, hopped out to retrieve the box, and carried it up the twelve steps to my front door. I offered to pay her for the kindness of going out of her way for a total stranger, but she refused my money.

After consulting with my friend, Marie Paule, about what might be the appropriate thing to do in France to repay her, I was told some chocolates would do.

In a few days, I returned to *La Poste* with a box of chocolate truffles as a token of my appreciation. She beamed as though it was the greatest present she had ever received.

Months later, I returned to *La Poste*. She was still talking about the chocolates I brought to her. Now years later, I feel compelled to write about her thoughtfulness.

She and her kindness showed me how people often have the wrong idea about French people.

How wrong it was to have preconceived ideas about a specific culture. It was arrogant to assume that people were a certain way. Kindness dissolved what can be perceived as arrogance.

SAN FRANCISCO RED BUTTER

Ingredients

1 pound butter, softened

8 cloves garlic, crushed

2 tablespoons Sweet Hungarian Paprika

1 tablespoon Worcestershire Sauce

Put all ingredients into a bowl and mix with a mixer until the butter is light and fluffy and all ingredients are well blended. Let stand for 24 hours to allow flavors to develop before using.

Use as a dip for breadsticks, crackers, or crostini. Can be used to dress cooked pasta or coat whitefish.

Stays fresh in a covered dish in the refrigerator for weeks.

The Marché

CHAPTER 4

Meeting Madame Campiston

*Discomfort is Part of Learning. Endure
Discomfort to Enrich Life.*

"*Cooking Class at Madame Campiston's*
Wednesday, November 10, 2012."

The poster was displayed on the receptionist's
desk at the Aix Language School where I was in my
fourth week of French classes. My heart leaped. Not
only would I immerse myself in an aspect of my newly
adopted country, but I would also get to cook in a real
French home.

Just the name, Madame Campiston, sounded impressive. I pictured her as someone well known. The way the
French used the term Madame had a ring of respect. Every
time I entered a store, and heard the clerk say, "*Bonjour,
Madame,*" I was thrilled. Everything about France seemed
exotic to me, even the most ordinary of things.

When I signed up for the class, I learned that Madame
Campiston was a great teacher of French cooking. She

lived in a house near the University of Aix, to which I could conveniently travel to by bus.

On Wednesday, at 5:30 I arrived at the *Rotonde* by *La Poste* bus stop where I would pick up the Number 4 bus. What a surprise! Jim and Steve, two of my fellow language classmates, were also waiting for a bus.

"You going to Madame Campiston's?" I asked.

"Yes," replied Steve. He and Jim were from Colorado on work permits to be on a ski patrol team in the French Alps. They needed French language lessons in order to perform their jobs. Steve was quite friendly and likable. Jim, on the other hand, was quiet and more distant.

"Your wife and son are not joining us?" I asked Steve.

"The class would keep my little one up too late. They are going to have dinner at home and watch TV."

Jim, in his typical manner, didn't say a thing. As a result, I didn't feel as connected with him.

When our bus arrived, we paid our fare and found our seats. We rode the bus through the city, passing many students on the streets, and kept our eyes peeled for our stop, at Churchill. After a while, however, the driver announced we were at the end of the line. Somehow, we didn't recognize our stop. Unfortunately, the driver did not know the area, as he was new on the job, and spoke no English. He could not give us directions to Madame Campiston's. Fortunately, Jim had come prepared with a map, and found we were not too far away. When he directed us to our destination, I reevaluated my opinion of Jim.

"Oh, if I'm going to get lost, I want to be with two ski *pisteurs*," I announced to them.

I called Madame Campiston on my cell phone and alerted her that we would be half an hour late.

My anticipation to actually see the inside of my first French house matched a young girl's eagerness for her first date. How exciting!

When we arrived at the home of Madame Campiston, a very petite French woman in her forties met us at the door. She had long, flowing dark brown hair and dark brown eyes and was dressed casually in jeans and a bright yellow tee shirt.

"We are here to see Madame Campiston," I proudly said.

She laughed and pointed to herself. *"Bonsoir, bienvenue chez moi."*

I was expecting an older woman with a buttoned-up dress, perfect makeup, and her hair tightly wound in a French roll. I remembered Madame Giry in Phantom of the Opera, the all-knowing, authoritative, demanding one. I chuckled at my silly preconception.

After introductions, I was eager to look around my first French home. The large living room had a red velvet couch and two Louis XIV upholstered chairs, one on each end of the couch. The coffee table, no doubt, was from another era, as it was dark wood heavily carved with ornate designs. Laden with books of various shapes and sizes, it gave the impression of someone who loved to read or be involved in a research project. A large, black pillar candle with white and tan stripes sat on one end of the table.

A treasure chest set off one wall. It too had carvings similar to the coffee table's and was made from the same dark wood. The pictures above the chest had very distinct images of plants and trees that had an unusual focus. The intriguing photographs were in black and white and depicted part of a leaf. The opposite wall displayed more black and white photographs hanging above a low piano. I later learned Madame Campiston's husband, Xavier, was an astute amateur photographer.

The dining room was an extension of this room and furnished very differently. The table and chairs, sleek and made with blond wood, had a modern look. It had been set for four with snow-white linens and simple patterned dishes, fancy silverware, and water and wine glasses. Petite bouquets of flowers, obviously from the garden, were placed on this table and in the kitchen. The home was decorated like a typical American home with a few French pieces. What a cozy place!

Our hostess took our coats and announced, "I have been instructed by the school to speak to you only in French, so please respond only in French."

Immediately I felt intimidated, realizing it would be a quiet night for me with my limited vocabulary.

"Great," responded Steve, while Jim nodded. Both were well advanced in the language.

The conversation then continued in French.

"*Que puis-je vous offrir a boire? Eau, café, the, ou du vin,*" said Madame Campiston looking directly at me. Thank goodness I knew she was asking if I wanted water, wine, coffee or tea to drink.

I needed all of my wits to utilize my limited French language to help me stay focused. Wine would obliterate what little French I knew, so I chose water. I stammered, "*L'eau, s'il vous plait.*"

Bill and Steve asked for wine.

Madame Campiston directed us to join her in the kitchen, *"Ce soir, nous allons faire de la soupe de carotte, une tarte de viande, une salade, et un gateau au chocolat."* Did she mean carrot soup, meat tart, salad, and chocolate?

Wait! She did say chocolate. Hooray—some cake!

"Nous allons commencer avec le gateau car il faut plus de temps a preparer."

Um, something about the cake; I thought she said it took a long time to make.

I scanned this French kitchen and saw an electric stove, a very small refrigerator, a dishwasher, a washing machine, but no clothes dryer or microwave. I later learned Madame Campiston liked to hang her laundry outside to dry and both Monsieur and Madame Campiston disliked microwaves.

Madame Campiston moved quickly around the kitchen, getting the ingredients and equipment needed for the chocolate cake. She named each item in French for our benefit. She held up the flour and said, *"Farine."* She held up a bag of sugar and said, *"Sucre,"* then the cocoa, *"Cacao,"* and lastly some eggs, *"Oeufs."*

She asked each of us, *"Quelle partie des Etats-Unis êtes vous?"*

When Jim and Steve named their hometowns in Colorado, I understood that she wanted to know what part of America we came from. I answered, "California."

"Qu'est ce qui vous améne á Aix?"

I pieced together that Jim and Steve spoke to her about their work exchange program with France but I didn't know what else they were saying. I remembered what I had learned in my French class that day. I took a deep breath, and said, "*J'étais ici* (I was here) *il y a trente ans avec mon mari* (thirty years ago with my husband). *Maintenant que je suis à la retraite* (Since I'm retired) *je peux revenir* (can return)." My words came out like a child who just learned to speak.

Madame Campiston slowed down her French so I could understand. "*Combien de temps allez-vous rester ici?*" I think she asked how long I would be in France.

"*Un an*," I said, "One year," adding in English, just to make sure.

Noticing my struggle with the language, she moved to English. "Perhaps after the holidays, you would like to meet with me for one hour each week so that I can practice my English and perhaps you would learn more French."

"I would like that very much," I replied, hoping she really meant it, as she had so much to teach. I wanted to become friends.

Our French cooking lesson continued. She put the cake batter in the oven and, just as at home, she offered the beaters and bowl for us to lick off the batter. She spoke in both French and English for my benefit.

Next she began cooking the carrots for the soup by placing them in a pan to boil on top of the stove. Then, out of the small refrigerator came the ingredients for the meat tart, which she put-in a frying pan.

Showing us a pastry package, she said, "You can buy this at the grocery store. You don't need to make it."

I thought this was a cooking class! I could also buy the carrot soup at the store.

She rolled out the pastry to the desired thickness and lined the tart pan, later putting in the cooked filling from the frying pan.

"Now that the cake is done, I will put the tart in to bake."

The carrots were also cooked, so she added some cumin and placed them in the blender to purée into soup.

After Madame Campiston made the salad, she invited us to sit at the table. "We will start with our entrée, carrot soup."

In France, the first course or starter was called an entrée. This confused me at first because in the United States, we called our main course the entrée. Once, I was asked to bring an entrée salad to a potluck and thinking it had to be the main course, I made one that included chicken.

I sat down across from Madame Campiston at the preset rectangular table. Jim sat at her left while Steve was at my right. We were offered more water and wine to go with our meal. I shuddered; *now the French conversation will begin while we are eating.*

Sure enough, Jim asked, "Madame Campiston, *ces plats sont typiquement français?*"

Did he just ask if these dishes were French? I gave him a puzzled look. She wouldn't be teaching us Italian recipes!

Madame added, "*Oui,*" and then to me in English, "Yes, I make each of them at least once a week, not always together, but at different meals."

Next Steve spoke in French, something about his wife.

Suddenly I had a flashback of being a child sitting at the dinner table, listening to the adults talking, knowing some of the words, but not understanding what was being said. I felt extremely insecure about not entering the conversation.

Finally, it was time to leave. I breathed a sigh of relief.

Madame Campiston gave us copies of the recipes of our meal — all in French, of course.

"*Bonne nuit, à bientôt,*" I called as we left, trying to leave her with an impression that I knew some French.

"*Bonne nuit,* Carine, I will call you after the holidays."

In January, the phone rang. "*Bonne année,* Carine, this is Marie Paule Campiston calling." With that announcement, Madame Campiston became Marie Paule to me, and over time became my very best friend in Aix. We saw each other at least twice a week to exchange language lessons and meals. Marie Paule called to check on my health and to drive me wherever I needed to go. I had lost count of the number of times she helped me navigate my way through French bureaucracy to solve a problem. She was never too busy and did not know the meaning of the word "no."

"You are the same age as my mother, but you are so different from her," Marie Paule said. "My mother doesn't do anything. You are so active and I can talk to you about anything."

She told me that her mother took the traditional role of French grandmothers who take care of the grandchildren. They must always be available, no matter the age of their children.

Over the year, I adopted the whole family. Her twelve-year-old daughter, Juliette, who was tall and thin with long blonde hair, won a place in my heart. A computer whiz, she was too shy to speak to me when we first met, but soon gave me a two-cheek kiss upon greeting me or saying goodbye. Xavier, Marie Paule's tall, thin, and handsome husband, was a *pedologue*, something similar to a podiatrist. He made house calls and twice a month came to my home to give me a pedicure or reflexology. I admired the confident way he went about his work as his long, thin fingers stroked my feet and toes. Oh, so relaxing. Always, I enjoyed the pampering. He even treated some of my visitors.

Whenever I spoke to Xavier on the phone, he said goodbye with, "I kiss you now."

When I first heard this, I thought he meant something intimate. Embarrassed, I did not want him to say that because he was the husband of my very best friend. It was only later that I realized his comment on the phone was the same as the two-cheek kiss that was so common in France as a way to say goodbye in person.

My best friend and her family had taught me to interact with my American family and friends with "I kiss you now," an endearing French way to say goodbye.

Being uncomfortable on the first evening at Madame Campiston's was a revelation to me.

Discomfort was part of learning, but learning enriched life.

I decided to endure discomfort.

Madame Campiston's Carrot Soup

Ingredients

2 1/4 pounds fresh carrots, sliced

1 chicken stock cube

2 cups water

Cumin to taste

1 cup crème fraîche or heavy whipping cream

Cook carrots in 2 cups of water with chicken stock cube. When the carrots are fork-tender, put into a blender with all the liquid and 1/2 cup of *crème fraîche*, and cumin, salt, and pepper to taste. Blend until smooth.

Whip the remaining 1/2 cup of *crème fraîche* until the whipped cream peaks. Fold in some cumin and place in the refrigerator until ready to use.

When ready to serve, place soup in bowls topped with a spoonful of cumin whipped cream.

This soup can be served cold in the summer or warm in the winter.

Bon Appetit!

CHAPTER 5

Not Too Old to Be a Mistress

Age is Not a Limitation

Monoprix was the grocery store where I shopped weekly for items I could not find at the fresh fruit and vegetable *marché*. One day I was checking out the fresh soups when I noticed a handsome man with tortoise shell-rimmed glasses standing beside me. He reached for a box of turnip soup. I stepped out of his way and continued with my shopping.

Later, I was at the checkout line when the cashier said, "*Avez-vous une carte de Monoprix?*"

Not understanding what she was asking I looked at her with a blank expression. She repeated the question.

From behind me, I heard a man's voice say in English, "Do you have a Monoprix card?"

I turned to see the handsome man from the soup aisle. He wore jeans and a black leather jacket. He stroked his dark hair streaked with gray and smiled at me.

Surprised, I muttered, "Thank you," to him, then turned to the clerk and shook my head, "No, I don't have a Monoprix card."

He moved closer as the clerk added up my purchases, "I assume you don't speak French," he said, "Where are you from?"

"California. I have only been here a few weeks."

"What brought you to Aix? California is such a beautiful place."

"I was looking for a change," I said, giving him a wink. "Do you know California?"

"I have been there, but I spend more time in Florida," he responded.

I wondered about Florida. "Are you retired?"

He feigned a hurt look and asked, "Do I look old enough to be retired?"

I made a quick repair to that *faux pas*. "Many people retire early these days."

"No, I'm a practicing doctor. My office is three doors down the street." He took a card out of his pocket and moved close to me. "You are new here and will have many questions. If there is anything you need, call me, I'll be happy to assist you." He peered directly in my eyes and handed me the card.

The clerk coughed to get my attention, then she asked for payment.

I paid for my shopping and thanked Mr. Handsome.

"It's been fun," he said. "I hope to see you very soon."

I giggled. "Yes, it was a pleasure to meet you. My name is Karin."

Later that evening, I reflected on how much fun we'd had. I resolved to call on him.

The next morning, I went to his office. There I encountered his receptionist who spoke no English.

Office front on Cours Mirabeau

"*Bonjour*," I said. I had learned nothing happened in France unless you used the magic word.

"*Bonjour. Puis-je vous aider?*" she said, smiling.

"I'd like to see Dr. Blaise."

"*Avez-vous un rendezvous?*"

I understood *rendezvous* as appointment. She probably wanted to know if I had an appointment. "No. He said I could come in anytime."

"*Avez-vous été référé par un autre médecin?*" I understood *autre médecin*. Did she ask if I was referred by another doctor?

My English was not getting us anywhere.

I showed her his card and wrote my name on the back and the word Monoprix. "Please give him this."

She took the card and disappeared into his office. Moments later, he appeared at the door. Smiling, he invited me into his exam room. "I'm happy to see you again." With a slight leer, he pointed to the consulting table where I could sit, while he sat behind his desk.

"Thank you for seeing me. I actually have a medical issue to consult with you. I get leg cramps at night and I am out of my quinine tablets, which require a prescription in the United States."

He seemed disappointed as he opened a desk drawer and pulled out a prescription pad.

"I am happy to write a prescription for you." He took off his little round glasses. "Anything else I can help you with?" This time there was a definite double entendre.

Armed with my lesson about discomfort, I took a leap. "Since I am new in town, I want to know where I might meet single men."

He came out from behind his desk and sat beside me on the exam table. "I am married, but my wife spends a lot of time in Florida." Peering over his tortoise shell spectacles, he said, "I'd like to see you privately."

"That's intriguing." I said, "But I don't date married men."

"But this is a common practice in France. All Frenchmen have mistresses, especially when one's wife is away so much."

"I am flattered, but I'm really looking for a single man."

He stood up from the exam table. The consultation was over. He put his arm around my shoulder and walked me out of the office to the front door, indicating that I wasn't to pay for the visit. He opened the door and said, "If you change your mind, you know where I am."

His parting words indicated his desire to see me.

Walking down my beloved Cours Mirabeau to the pharmacy to get my prescription filled, I chuckled that I had just been propositioned to be the mistress of a much younger and very handsome medical doctor.

In this wonderful country, age didn't matter. Ooh la la.

Cream of Turnip Soup
Very popular in France

Ingredients

2 Tablespoons unsalted butter

1 small onion, diced

2 pounds turnips, trimmed, peeled and diced

1 1/2 cups chicken stock

1 1/2 cups bottled water

2 dried bay leaves

fine sea salt

1/4 cup *crème fraîche*

Place the butter, onion, and turnips in a large, heavy-bottomed saucepan over medium heat and cook until the onions and turnips are translucent, stirring occasionally so they don't stick, for about 15 minutes. Add the stock and the water, stir, and add the bay leaves and salt to taste. Increase the heat to medium-high and bring to a boil. Reduce the heat so the liquid is at a lively simmer and cook, covered, until the turnips are very tender, 25 to 30 minutes.

Remove the bay leaves and puree the soup. Whisk in the *crème fraîche* so the soup is slightly foamy. Season to taste with salt, and serve.

Makes 4 to 6 servings

CHAPTER 6

Pétanque

*Confidence Grows with the
Desire to Succeed*

Close to the center of small villages, groups of men
gathered together under the shade of the typical French
plane trees, which incidentally were not plain, on a gravelly court, playing a game. The men, aged between sixty
and seventy years, were very intent on what they were
doing. They spoke little but appeared to have a strong
camaraderie. As I watched, I could see they were playing *petanque*, a game originated in the south of France
in the early 1900s.

For my French acculturation to be complete, I needed
to learn the game, even though it was typically played
by men. That never stopped me. Perhaps that was my
motivation. However, I found a group in Aix that played
weekly and welcomed me as a single woman. Soon
thereafter, Sunday mornings were reserved for *petanque*, a game I was intent on mastering. I had become

familiar with it on my previous travels to France with Bill. It was played with three heavy steel balls the size of tennis balls and a small wooden ball on a narrow, uneven, gravelly court about forty feet long. When I joined a *petanque* group in November, I learned the finer points of the game.

We played on the public *Boules Courts*, just off the Rue Peripherique, close to Hotel Roi Rene and Parc Jordan. As I had noticed in the other towns, the courts were surrounded with plane trees. The green foliage provided shade from the fierce summertime Provençal sun. Half of the eight players who attended regularly, weather permitting, were women.

On my first morning, four of us turned up to play. I immediately noticed Paul, a handsome single Frenchman with a thick head of white hair and intense blue eyes. Unfortunately, he was not paired with me. John, one of the regulars, had the bad luck to be my partner and teach me about the game. He and his wife Betty, both Americans, had lived in Aix for three years and had plenty of practice. John wore blue Bermuda shorts and a darker blue sweater vest over a white polo shirt. He was heavyset with a jovial personality while Betty seemed serious, dressed in designer clothes from top to bottom.

Betty eyed me as a new woman partnering with her husband John. She seemed to be sizing me up.

He showed me the *cochonnet*, the table tennis-size wooden ball. "One person throws it out and then we take turns tossing one steel ball at a time to see who can come closest to the *cochonnet*. After each team member has thrown all three of their balls, the person whose ball came closest is declared the winner and receives a point." He winked at me. "That will be us."

"Seems like an easy game," I lied, covering up my lack of confidence.

John laughed. "Don't let it fool you. The unevenness of the court can cause all kinds of diversions. When you think you're the closest, an experienced opponent can strike the winning ball out of the way."

He instructed me how to stand inside the circle drawn with a stick in the dirt by the starting person. He showed me how to bend my knees and keep my back straight. Then came the hard part.

"Hold the ball under one hand, keep your eye on the *cochonnet*, and toss the ball underhanded with a flick of the wrist in an upward motion."

John, the teacher, threw out the *cochonnet* twenty-five feet to get the game started. He then tossed one of his balls.

Betty strutted and stepped inside the circle. She twirled her first ball with a spin. It veered away from the *cochonnet*, "Oh, darn!"

John turned to me. "It's your turn, partner."

"Okay, no problem." Overwhelmed with all of the instructions, I pitched the ball. It went far beyond the *cochonnet* and any of the other balls. "Wow. That went wild."

"Don't worry, Karin. You'll get better."

I watched closely as the others took their turns trying to get close to the *cochonnet*. Some threw with a spin, others with a curve.

Petanque at its best

My next throw came more easily. With beginner's luck, I suddenly appeared to be in first place. "Oh well, this isn't so tough."

Betty groaned and playfully kicked the dirt.

Paul came next in line. He threw the ball high into the air to avoid a gully and some rocks on the court. His ball landed precisely on top of my winning ball, knocking it out of the competition.

I felt violated! *How dare he.*

"Nice shot, Paul," shouted Betty. She high-fived him.

What would you expect from a Frenchman who probably played *petanque* most of his life.

Paul's ball was now closest to the *cochonnet*. John and I sneered.

John said, "Let's see what I can do." He stepped inside the circle, took his time, and threw the perfect shot next to the *cochonnet*.

"That's my partner," I boasted.

"I hope it's good enough, partner," John replied. He stepped out of the circle to allow Betty to step in for her throw.

She threw one of her famous curved balls but hit Paul's ball slightly away from its former winning spot.

"Oh, no," she moaned.

When John and I cheered, she glared at her husband.

Paul walked over to the balls. "Too close to call," he pronounced. "We'll need to measure this one."

He returned to his bag, pulled out a string with a pointed plastic arrow at each end, and walked back to the controversial balls. He bent down so that he could measure the distance between his ball and the *cochonnet*. He then measured the distance between John's ball and the little orb. Paul's ball was closer by half an inch.

"This is serious business," I said.

Paul looked at me and smiled, as if saying, *I bet you wish you were on my team.*

I nodded at the handsome Frenchman.

"One point for Betty and Paul," John called out. He glanced at me so that I would understand the score.

Betty pursed her lips with pride.

Starting the next round, Betty tossed the *cochonnet* and then her ball, which landed a foot away from a winning spot.

When it was my turn, I aimed with beginner's precision and threw the ball. It rolled into the rocks and twigs on the court, making it go a long way from the *cochonnet*.

"Darn, I have a wild ball," I exclaimed.

"Don't worry, it's only a game," said John.

At that point, I secretly named him "Adorable John."

He informed me, "The game goes to thirteen points and then we switch partners."

Did he sound a little relieved that he would have a new partner?

"We usually play for two hours, then go to Le Grillon for *pastis*, a traditional French aperitif," chimed in Paul. "The losers pay."

I guessed that he seldom paid.

With each throw, my confidence grew, just like anything else that I took on, such as moving to France. My desire to succeed and my concentration paid dividends. I got closer to the *cochonnet* with more throws, and surprisingly, was having fun doing it.

When we switched partners, I joined Paul's side. At one point, he put his arm around my waist to show me his winning stance. I liked being the newcomer getting attention from the men.

As I had predicted, at the end of two hours of play, Paul had the highest number of points, assuring yet again that he wouldn't be paying for the *pastis*.

I knew that practice and my desire to succeed would improve my game. However, I always had to pay for the pastis.

But if at first you don't succeed, ask a seasoned petanque player to show you his winning stance.

DIY Pastis

Ingredients

10 star anise pods

1 tablespoon licorice root

1/2 teaspoon fennel seeds

1/2 teaspoon coriander

1/4 teaspoon anise seeds

1 1/2 cups vodka

1/3 cup sugar

1/2 cup water

With a mortar and pestle, roughly break up star anise, licorice root, fennel, coriander, and anise. Add them to a sealable glass jar along with vodka. Seal and shake, then let steep for five days at room temperature away from direct sunlight, shaking occasionally.

At the end of five days, boil sugar and water together until integrated into a light syrup, about seven minutes. While the syrup is cooling, strain the spices out of the vodka mixture through a cheesecloth lining a fine-mesh strainer. Strain twice if necessary to remove all sediment.

Once syrup is cool, add it to the strained vodka infusion and shake. Let rest for four days or more before use. Store at room temperature for up to four months.

When ready to serve, serve in a small pitcher along with a glass of ice for each person. Individuals can pour as much as they like over the ice and then top with water.

Fall comes to Aix and Roi Rene

CHAPTER 7

Old Traditions and New

"Acknowledging the good that you already have in your life is the foundation for all abundance."

Eckhart Tolle

"*Are you going to the* Thanksgiving Dinner?"

"Thanksgiving here in France? What are you talking about?" I asked Paul. We walked side by side after *petanque* over to Le Grillon for *pastis*. We left the tree-shaded boules court and stepped onto the sidewalk, which was lined with seventeenth-century three-story stone buildings.

When we reached the bistro close to the *boules* court, I asked, "Can you tell me about the dinner?"

"The Anglo-American Group of Provence (AAGP) put on an annual Thanksgiving Dinner. It will be next Sunday. I can pick you up at *La Rotonde* and take you in my car if you'd like," said Paul as we were nearing the bistro.

How could I refuse my first invitation to an adventure since moving to France, and with a single man?

"I'd love to go." I secretly gave myself a high-five for this coup.

Paul led me into the quiet bistro where Betty and John were sitting at a gray-and-white marble-topped table. They motioned to us to join them.

Paul announced, "Karin is joining us for Thanksgiving."

Betty seemed relieved that a man other than her husband was interested in me. "I've trained the chefs at the French Restaurant Le Verguetier," she said. "They prepare a traditional dinner just as we would at home. When we first began twenty-years ago, they didn't know how to stuff and roast a turkey or what cranberries were, much less how to make sauce from them. The only thing they did with a pumpkin was to make soup. So of course, they didn't know how to make a pumpkin pie." She turned up her nose. "Their first attempts had few spices and the filling was only half an inch thick! With my supervision, their pies turned into mouthwatering desserts." She smacked her lips.

I rolled my eyes at Paul. Speaking of desserts, I looked at Paul. "I can't wait. This will be my first holiday away from home and family."

During the week, I anticipated the Thanksgiving dinner. I chose my dress, one with long sleeves in a black and beige color. In California, going to an event with people I didn't know would have been nerve-racking. I would have fretted about being dressed appropriately and measuring up to the other women. That didn't even enter my mind here. I was so eager for new experiences that I was not at all anxious as I waited at the *Rotonde* for Paul to arrive.

A gray Prius pulled up and Paul hopped out to greet me. Dressed in a blue button-down dress shirt and a brown tweed sports jacket, he gave me the customary French two-cheek kiss. I handed him a bottle of Champagne as a gift for the ride. He opened the door for me and off we went to the restaurant.

Fifty people had already arrived when we got there. The large room had seven round tables with ten place settings each and a centerpiece with fall-colored leaves, small pumpkins, and nuts, just like at home. I laughed at a table reserved as the "Kids' Table."

Since I knew only the seven from my *petanque* group, I began introducing myself to others in the room. I felt the excitement of the long-time members with their anticipation of the annual dinner with many familiar friends. I was excited too, but for me, it was because of so many new faces and being there with Paul. I was relieved that I had dressed appropriately, as I noted the other women had similar dressy fall attire. They seemed relaxed as they held drinks and laughed with friends.

I flashed back to the time I moved with Bill to San Francisco twenty-seven years earlier. He had taken the position as CEO at an electronics company in South San Francisco, and I was taking a year off from my private counseling practice in Southern California. It was one of the loneliest years of my life. As a psychotherapist, I knew that having a purpose in one's life led to happiness and fulfillment; however I had focused on the fact that it was the first time since having and raising children that I wasn't working or going to graduate school. The luxury of a year without demands on my time blinded me to the potential pitfalls of a life of leisure. That isolated year in the Bay Area made me realize I didn't know how to reach out to make friends. During childhood, I had moved frequently with my family. My mother, trying to better her situation, chose a new school district each year. I became so discouraged at leaving one school after another that I stopped making new friends.

I was determined to make this year very different from those lonely days in San Francisco.

When Paul left to get drinks, John approached me. "How nice to see you, Karin," he said. Not far behind was Betty, grabbing his elbow, spilling part of his wine. But he continued, "You look very nice tonight."

"Why, thank you. You've only seen me dressed for *petanque*. I'm glad you like my dress."

Betty nudged John, spilling the rest of his wine. John just looked at Betty and brushed the wine off his sleeve.

Paul returned and handed me a glass of Champagne. "You didn't get one for yourself?" I wondered if that because he was driving? "No," he said, "We should find a spot to sit before all the seats are taken." He steered me toward one table, while Betty pulled John off to another one.

The people at the table were either French or English and had lived in Aix for a long time.

"Yes, I moved to Aix for nine months, twenty-eight years ago," reported Susan, a petite blonde American; that made us all laugh, though it seemed to be a common experience here. Sitting next to Susan was her friend,

Debbie, a slightly overweight dark-haired woman from North Carolina.

One Frenchwoman's husband was from Holland; another American woman's husband was French; while another Englishwoman sported an Irish mate. Never had I been in such an international group. My circle of friends back home in Orange County was a homogeneous group who had lived there most of their lives and thought pretty much alike. Even though the conversation dwelt on where everyone was from and how long they had lived in Aix, I felt alive with the diversity.

The chefs brought out large turkeys, one for each table. We needed to designate our own carver. "Oh no, not me," were the words whispered around the table. Helen, the Englishwoman, drew the short straw and good-naturedly took on the task.

Donning an apron and gloves, Helen picked up a very large carving knife and fork, and began with confidence, much to our encouragement and cheers. We clinked our glasses filled with French wine and said, "*À Helen*." She carefully placed each slice of turkey on a platter to be passed around the table. Steaming bowls of mashed potatoes, mashed sweet potatoes, green beans, and a rich turkey gravy arrived from the kitchen. Bowls of chestnut stuffing from the turkey and cranberry sauce were passed around. Baskets of sliced baguettes and bottles of rosé and red wine completed the meal. What a bountiful French-American Thanksgiving meal!

The platter of turkey reached me and I offered it to Paul.

I couldn't resist asking, "Do you like the breast meat or a thigh?"

"I'll take some of that white meat," he chuckled.

"The French really know how to cook," I observed. I had never eaten such moist turkey, not even my own.

As I took a bite of the mashed potatoes laden with butter, I glanced at Paul. He was rolling some around in his mouth as though he was savoring the morsel. He caught me looking at him and winked.

Oh, I do like the fun of playing with this Frenchman!

Just as in America, the Thanksgiving meal was over way too soon. We all groaned with the pleasure and suffering of having eaten too much, when the now famous pumpkin pies arrived with a generous bowl of whipped cream for topping. Despite being stuffed, no one turned down the fabulous pumpkin pies.

I passed the bowl of whipped cream to Paul. "Do you like your cream whipped?"

He winked again. "Mmm. It's best that way."

We stood to leave; Paul squeezed my hand and gave me a smile. For the long-timers living in Aix, Thanksgiving was coming to a close, but for me, I had just opened my life to a year of pleasure.

The next day, my telephone rang and I heard a French accent.

"Hello, Carine, you don't know me, but I am Arlette, a friend of Paul's. He wants to share the bottle of Champagne you gave him at my apartment tonight. He likes to entertain at my place."

I hesitated a moment then said, "Sure. I'd like to come." I wrote down the details. "*Tres bien*, I'll see you tonight." How generous of him to share, I thought, but who was this woman caller? If she was his girlfriend, why wasn't she at the dinner last night? My mind began to imagine all sorts of things in this unfamiliar culture. What kind of evening was this to be? Surely, it wouldn't be a threesome? But then again it was France. *Viva la différence?* I didn't want this to be part of my new adventure. Otherwise, I'd have to choose my clothing very carefully!

When I arrived at Arlette's that evening, I was relieved to discover that Susan and Debbie were also there. Thank goodness, there would be no *ménage à trois* tonight. During the evening I discovered that Arlette was a very good friend of Paul's, but not a girlfriend. Truly, Paul didn't like to entertain, but enjoyed the opportunity created to share the bottle. He didn't drink Champagne, but he relished his Scotch whiskey.

As pleasant as the evening was, I had no desire to flirt with Paul. I needed a way to handle my disappointment. Quickly, I recognized what I frequently told my clients, that when life presented a challenge, with time, an opportunity would present itself. My opportunity would be a year of exploration and pleasure. Also, Susan and Debbie would become good friends.

Thanksgiving in America was traditionally celebrated surrounded with family and friends. Family can be new friends wherever I was. Here on my adventure, I had discovered a new family in the Anglo-American Group of Provence.

I still planned to live my adventure of pleasure.

Paul's Mashed Potatoes

Ingredients

2 pounds yellow fingerlings or Yukon gold potatoes

1 pound butter, cold

1/4 cup milk

salt to taste

Place unpeeled potatoes in a pot and cover with water. Bring to a boil, then reduce heat to a rapid simmer and cook for 35 to 40 minutes or until tender. Drain and peel. Transfer to a bowl and let potatoes cool slightly.

Turn potatoes through a food mill on the finest setting, then place back into the cooking pot. Heat pot over medium heat, stirring until heated through and steam begins to come off the bottom of the pot. Add butter in 5 portions, allowing each portion of butter to be almost melted before adding the rest, until it has all been incorporated.

Warm the milk to lukewarm. Stir in the warm milk until combined. Using a whisk, vigorously stir potatoes until fluffy. Season with salt.

Smooth the top of the potatoes with the back of a spoon or an offset spatula.

Try to stop licking the spoon.

Makes 5 1/2 cups, or, about 6 servings.

CHAPTER 8

Meeting Mark the Expat

*Bliss May Be Around the
Corner. Be Open to Romance.*

There he was, just one of four men in the group. There were fifteen participants who sat at the Poetry Evening at Book in Bar, the only English bookstore in Aix-en-Provence. He sat there looking content, with reddish brown hair, not particularly handsome. He was probably in his early sixties, with a paunch, but he had the kindliest brown eyes I had seen since those of my husband Bill. I took my seat while Sheila, the group leader, started the meeting by asking us to introduce ourselves. The individuals were a diverse group from England, Ireland, France, United States, Holland, Sweden, and Scotland.

The man with kind eyes, Mark, was a former literature teacher in a private girls' school in England, now retired and living in Aix. Literature! My first major as an undergraduate, so I was even more intrigued.

When it was time for me to tell my story, I said, "I am now an *Aixois*."

Someone in the group corrected me, "Be careful, a female is an *Aixoise*," emphasizing the pronunciation.

In my first meeting, I quickly learned this group was precise and not afraid to show it. I glanced over at Mark. He looked back at me with his gentle eyes.

During the meeting, I kept gazing at Mark and his kind eyes showing softness, contentment, and an openness.

The time passed quickly. After the meeting, I navigated my way over to Mark to introduce myself in a respectable way. We made small talk before the whole group took off to Bastide du Cours, a local bistro, for an *apéro*.

In the restaurant, Mark came over to sit by me. I was delighted to have the attention. Evidently my French blunder didn't label me as someone to be avoided. I learned that not only did Mark have kindly eyes, but he took an interest and listened attentively. How refreshing!

"What brought you to Aix?" he began.

I told my story about being here thirty years ago on my honeymoon when my husband and I fell in love with Aix. "I promised myself I would return."

Mark looked around the bistro. "Is he here with you?"

"Unfortunately, he died several years ago."

"My condolences. But you came anyway?"

"Yes, I had to keep that promise to myself. It became my dream to live in France."

Our two-way conversation ended when others intruded by talking about poetry.

But before the evening came to an end, Mark asked if I'd like to have dinner the next evening.

Are you kidding? At that point, I had been in France for seven weeks and here was a single man in my age range showing an interest in me.

"Love to! Where shall we meet?"

We arranged the meeting place and time before we said good-bye using the customary French double-cheek kiss.

On my walk home, I thought about how pleasant it was to have the attention of a kind-eyed man who listened and wanted to take me out to dinner. I yearned for this kind of companionship.

The following evening we met as arranged at the first natural spring fountain on Cours Mirabeau. We walked to the nearby *centre ville* restaurant, Chez Mitch, as neither of us had a car.

The small restaurant was elegantly appointed with white tablecloths. When seated, we were handed menus in French. Mark helped me read it, because I was only in my fourth week of French lessons. I ordered *Dorade grillée farcie aux tomates et basilic* (white fish with tomatoes and basil) while he decided on the *Côtes d'agneau farcie aux truffes* (lamb chops with truffles).

I shared that I was a retired Marriage and Family Therapist.

He reacted by asking, "Should I be on my guard?"

"No, I'm not analyzing you or anyone. Remember, I am retired. Besides, I always valued the wisdom of literature more than the revelations that have come from the field of psychology. You, as an English major, must agree that authors know more about human behavior."

"I believe that, too. They really understand the human condition."

He sipped his wine. "How'd you like to get out of town?" he asked suddenly. "We could hire a car and go to the Mediterranean."

"Do you mean rent a car?" I asked.

"Yes, we could drive, couldn't we?"

I discovered that "hire" to an Englishman meant "to rent" to an American. We made a plan to check out Hertz and Avis the next day.

After dinner, Mark walked me home. As we were strolling along to my apartment, I wondered about the correct protocol in France of inviting a man up to my apartment. As nice as it felt to walk arm in arm, I made my decision based on my American Three-Date Rule. I had always relied on my decision to postpone any intimacy until we had known each other for at least three dates. It had served me well and in this case, avoided any possible misunderstanding in this foreign culture. We said goodnight at my door with another French two-cheek kiss.

The next day, we arranged to rent a car for several days later in the week. In the meantime, we met daily for coffee in one of the many outdoor cafés on Cours Mirabeau and talked and laughed about life.

My three-date rule satisfied, I invited him to dinner at my apartment. I prepared a favorite of mine, *coq au vin*, and served it along with a baguette and a bottle of red wine. The evening went by in our low-key way, but I realized our friendship was developing. A warm feeling went through me as I realized eight weeks ago I didn't know a soul in this foreign country. I was also aware that even though Mark and I both spoke English, there was still a language barrier, since many words differed in English and American English.

On Friday, we picked up our little Italian Fiat. After signing the paperwork, we decided I would be the driver while Mark navigated. We'd brought driver licenses, credit cards, a map, and we each had a fifty-euro bill for spending money. It was a beautiful sunny day and we were set to go!

Mark wanted to show me Sainte-Maxime, a village and small port on the Mediterranean where he once docked his boat. He knew the way and made an excellent navigator for my first driving experience in France on the toll road.

The first payment station took all of our combined 9.70 euros in change. We paid and were off again on the impeccably maintained road.

Once we left the toll road and took the smaller road to the coast, we crossed the Massif des Maures mountain range on a winding route before we dropped into the small seaside village of Sainte-Maxime. With only 13,500 inhabitants, it was popular with artists, poets, and writers who enjoyed the climate and were attracted by the azure blue water. The old town faced the small harbor and housed the typical tourist fare of cafés, souvenir shops, and the beach.

We walked to the port. On the way, we saw a war memorial commemorating the landing spot of the invasion and liberation of Southern France during World War II. The Germans actually gave up their stronghold here to the United States "Attack Force Delta" on August 15, 1944.

Once at the harbor, Mark showed where his boat had been docked before he sold it. He told me some of his adventures at sea, when suddenly he had an idea.

"I wanted to take you to Saint-Tropez on the ferry, but it isn't running in the winter. In summer it is the only decent way to get there as the road is jammed with tourists. Now we'll have to drive."

"That shouldn't be a problem now, should it?" I asked, pleased he wanted to take me to Saint-Tropez, a place I had always heard about.

We headed back to the car and began the drive to Saint-Tropez, the town made famous by Brigitte Bardot and her yellow, polka-dotted bikini. The road was narrow and lined with pine trees that reminded me of the area around Carmel, California.

"This drive is so picturesque with single estates and houses lining the road," I commented. "I could live here."

"I could live here, too. It is the only beach area on the Côte d'Azur that has done it right by not allowing a multitude of high-rise apartment buildings."

As we approached Saint-Tropez, large yachts docked in the marina came into view. They were grander and more plentiful than I had seen before. The area attracted the rich and famous! Once in Saint-Tropez, we parked the car. We walked around the old town, which was closed to traffic. With its ocher-colored buildings, it was charming and also the only place I had seen an upscale boutique next to a family grocery store. Unfortunately, I could not view the merchandise; the village was closed down. November was a month-long vacation for many shops and restaurants.

Mark wanted to take me to a classy restaurant. He was disappointed to discover it was also closed. We found a place humming with chatter and filled with locals who all appeared to know each other. We ordered local fish and a pitcher of rosé. The lunch was just fine and reminded me of what Bill always said, "It's impossible to get a bad meal in France."

After lunch, we walked across the parking lot to le Musée de l'Annonciade, an art museum housed in a sixteenth-century chapel now owned by the city of Saint-Tropez. It was open.

Inside, I noted the pristine white walls made the perfect frame for the views of the waterfront out each window. Each scene competed with the artwork, but as I looked, I was amazed that such a small art museum contained so many original Provençal impressionist and pointillist paintings. Surprises like this were one of the reasons I loved living in France.

We spent an hour viewing the paintings of Paul Signac, a pointillist who had resided in Saint-Tropez. One picture stood out to me. It was of a woman dressed in white standing barefoot in the shallow surf. Her diaphanous dress, perhaps wet with foam, allowed her breasts and figure to be suggestively revealed.

I enjoyed the picture so long that Mark purchased a small print for me to take home and suggested, "We could visit the nude beach, but we might find it to be empty."

"I'm only interested in going if you agree to take off your clothes first," I teased. We laughed. I really didn't want to see his bulging tummy!

Instead of the nude beach, we drove back to Aix. We arrived at the tollbooth with no small change, having used what we had on the way to Sainte-Maxime.

Mark faced the closed gate. "I believe the machine takes credit cards."

The automated pay station rejected both of our cards. The gate stood defiant. Cars backed up behind us. Mark called on the emergency telephone on the booth and spoke in French, explaining our problem.

He turned to me. "The operator says to insert one of our 50-euro bills for our 9.70 euro charge." We did as instructed.

Suddenly, it sounded as though we had hit the jackpot at Monte Carlo! *Ka-Ching, ka-ching, ka-ching*, as the difference between the 9.70 toll charge and the 50-euro bill came rushing out in two-euro coins. The coins spilled out onto the pavement, making it necessary to get out of the car to pick them up.

The sound of the coins took me back to Monte Carlo while on my honeymoon. My always confident husband suggested we go into the casino. Dressed in my warm-up suit, I begged off.

"But how often will you have this opportunity?" Bill insisted. "We are only here for the night."

With that, I pulled myself up to my full height of five foot two inches, held my head up high, and strode in with the dignity of Princess Grace along with my equally regal prince into the Monte Carlo. We walked past all of the elegantly dressed gamblers straight to the room with slot machines. We had only put in five coins when I heard the music all gamblers long to hear.

Ka-ching, ka-ching, ka-ching. The French francs just poured out of our machine! A tuxedoed employee rushed to my side with a very large paper cup into which I put our winnings. He said something in French I didn't understand, probably indicating how I could exchange that container for paper money, but I was too mortified with the attention being drawn to me to understand. Very quickly, my handsome prince and I ran to the nearest exit, giggling all the way!

Back with Mark, I laughed hysterically as the gate rose up, freeing us to make our exit. A usually jovial Mark grew serious. "Please, Karin, stop your laughing and pay attention to your driving."

I felt as though water had been thrown on me. I chalked it up to yet another experience in my new land.

Back at Aix, Mark and I purchased gas with the 40.30 in two-euro coins, relieving my purse of its heavy load! The surprised attendant must have thought we hit a jackpot somewhere.

We returned the car to the rental agency, and the clerk asked if we had any trouble. We burst out laughing, remembering the toll and coins. We left her wondering what had we been drinking.

During our walk back to my apartment on the cold November night, we walked arm and arm. Mark's nose began to dribble. The hairs hanging from his nose were so long, he needed a barber. The dripping clung to the hair—creating a stalagtite! How do you tell a man to wipe his nose? I said nothing and at some point I noticed it magically disappeared!

Not wanting to end the day, I invited Mark over for an impromptu dinner of Brussels sprouts from the *marché* and *lardon* with an omelette, accompanied by a baguette and a bottle of wine.

After dinner, when we were seated on the large sectional couch in my living room, myself at one end and Mark ten feet away under bright lights. The *ba boom, ba boom* reverberated from the disco below. He calmly asked, "I don't suppose you'd be interested in having a sexual relationship?"

I was shocked and confused at his statement, especially remembering his dripping nose and bulging tummy. The suddenness and the businesslike manner in which the question was posed made it difficult for me to give it the attention it deserved. Was this a British non-romantic way of approaching this subject? If so, it hardly made me feel desired.

I liked our relationship just the way it was, two playmates who spent a lot of time together, laughing and talking about anything and everything. I was too focused on the newness of my year's adventure and thoughts of Bill to think of beginning a romance.

I spared his feelings, "Mark, I am at the stage of life that having a good friend like you means more to me than a sexual one."

"I'll take that as a no," came his unemotional comment.

"Yes," was all I could muster.

After that evening, we saw less of each other. I missed his company and imagined he was moving on to another conquest. Something else was going on that

I would discover at the next poetry session. However, we did get together prior to that meeting.

"Mark, I am going to the Saint Lucia Day Festival of Light on December 13 at the Cathedral Saint-Saveur. Would you like to go with me?" I asked.

"I don't know anything about it. Tell me more," he said.

I told him about the Scandinavian tradition celebrated on what was once thought to be the longest night of the year. The event was about the struggle between light and darkness, something the Swedes know a lot about. The Swedish students who were in Aix-en-Provence studying the French language were putting it on. I wanted to see them in traditional costume sing both the procession and later, Christmas carols in Swedish. I had heard about this tradition from my Swedish grandmother when I was a little girl.

"It sounds interesting, I'll go," he replied.

We made our plans to meet that evening at the Cathedral. We greeted each other and then entered the old dimly lit twelfth-century building where we found seats in the wooden choir pews that lined both sides of the sanctuary. Beeswax candles burned from the various altars.

A hush of whispered voices permeated the vast, cavernous church. I sat in awe of the centuries-old cathedral.

Suddenly, the lights went out and the church became black. As our eyes adjusted to the darkness, a slight flicker of light appeared at the main entrance. Voices could faintly be heard singing the Neapolitan tune of Saint Lucia, but in the Swedish language. The light became brighter and the voices louder and more distinct as the procession approached. We could now see the leader dressed in all-white robe with a vivid red sash around her waist. On her head was a crown of green leaves and three lighted white candles. Behind her was a line of young women also dressed in white with a red sash, but carrying one tall, lighted taper. All were singing the traditional song. The audience hushed as they walked slowly by.

When the girls arrived at the altar, Saint Lucia stood in the middle, facing us while the other young women formed a line around her. They all proceeded to sing five Swedish Christmas carols.

When finished, they repeated the procession out the door and down the street to the Hotel de Ville where traditional grog and cookies were served.

While Mark and I made the procession through the village to the hotel, I felt I was in a foreign film, walking with the young ladies in costume with only the light from candles illuminating the way for the hundreds of attendees. I said a silent prayer, thanking Bill for giving me the opportunity to be here, participating in a tradition of my ancestors.

Two weeks later, another Poetry Night was held again at Book in Bar.

It was the December meeting, and Sheila had asked each of us to write a poem and be prepared to read it. In the spirit of participating in the group, I prepared one even though I didn't consider myself a poet. The Christmas market and lights on the plane trees running up my beloved Cours Mirabeau provided my inspiration. Several others went first with their poetry, which almost intimidated me, but I decided to go ahead anyway.

Christmas on Cours Mirabeau

Cours Mirabeau that greatest of seducers
Has captivated me for thirty years
I will always remember those plane trees
With branches outstretched
Stretching, swaying, dancing in the wind
Like lovers eager to touch across the boulevard
Many years later here I am
Still bewitched by those outstretched arms
Now decked out with lights of Noel
Christmas Market below beckoning throngs of
shoppers
Milling, looking, imagining
The timeless dream of finding the perfect gift
On Cours Mirabeau

I looked up as I finished and was pleasantly surprised by the applause and apparent acceptance of my poem. It gave me the courage to promise myself to write in the coming year.

We went around the room with poets reading their creations. When it was Mark's turn, he declined, even though I knew he had written a piece inspired by the traditional Santa Lucia program we had attended.

When everyone finished, Mark shook his head and asked Sheila if he might volunteer something.

She responded, "Please."

He stood up and walked across the room until he was standing beside me, gathered his thoughts, and spoke to the entire room. Mark began reciting from memory T. S. Elliot's "Journey of the Magi," a recital which lasted at least ten minutes. He dramatized and gave his performance all of the agitation the narrator felt. His audience was spellbound, including me. I had no idea he had this within him, even though I knew he was a literature professor. He finished with a nod of his head, wished everyone a Merry Christmas, and walked quietly back to his seat. The room broke out in a spontaneous applause.

When the meeting ended, all the women in the room swarmed around Mark to give him the recognition he deserved. They discovered that this intense man was full of knowledge, and able to express the poetry he loved. Why had they not been entranced a month earlier by his kindly eyes? Was this something that my thirty years of seeing qualities in people, that caring eyes were a revelation of the soul? In the moment, I forgot his weight and was ready to explore this man's passion.

When his moment of glory passed, Mark approached me. "I need to talk to you."

He invited me to have an *apero* on Cours Mirabeau.

Sitting at the bistro, we drank our wine. Mark became pensive. "I am going back to London tomorrow. My elderly parents need me. I will not be back and I won't be seeing you again."

I felt devastated. I couldn't comprehend what he was saying and more importantly, I realized for the first time just how much he meant to me.

"You can't mean it; you can't just leave like this. We need to talk about this," came my desperate plea.

"We can meet for breakfast, if you like."

Women from the poetry meeting arrived and hovered around him. This was no place for a conversation.

"Okay," I agreed.

I spent a sleepless night, wondering just what I wanted from another meeting with Mark. I was surprised by the depth of my feelings and the abandonment I felt after knowing Mark for only four weeks. I calmed down by reminding myself I was alone in a foreign country, I did not speak the language, and I had left my family and all of my friends behind. No wonder I became attached so quickly to Mark. Recognizing the symptoms of my isolation, I began to understand what I wanted when I met with Mark. I wanted to know what I meant to him. I wanted to know that the time we spent together was as important to him as it was to me.

We met for breakfast at a café. Mark seemed nervous. "I am sorry about the abruptness of my leaving," he began. He went on with some vague descriptions of a family problem. I wondered if he'd run away from something. I'd heard that many expats left for other countries to recover. Indeed, I was here recovering from my true love's death.

"Mark, I need to know what I mean to you," I ventured. He avoided my request and continued to talk about his upcoming departure. This was not like him to not hear what I had to say.

Feeling our time slipping away, I became even more determined. "Mark, there is one thing I want to know before you leave. Please tell me, what do I mean to you?"

He hesitated, giving it some thought. "I have always found you to be a good and kind person." A typical understated and, to me, very British answer.

I was hoping to hear, "I loved you and our time together." Now I was the nervous one and couldn't wait to end this breakfast and say the inevitable goodbye.

We stood, and gave a heartfelt hug and a kiss. Instead of the two-cheek French buss, to my surprise, Mark initiated a lover's kiss. Finally, a romantic moment. But why now?

He headed off in his direction. I walked back to my apartment, holding back my tears.

Two weeks of emptiness encouraged me to tell my friend Ruth Malone about my experience and how I was feeling.

She provided me with an insight I would never forget. "Karin, you are living in a foreign land filled with expats. You must remember that they come and they go. You have two choices. The first is to protect your heart and never reach out again to an expat, or secondly, make friends with them, knowing they will eventually leave. Just enjoy whatever time you have with them."

As Ruth talked, I realized she was telling me more than just how to think about expats abroad. It was a metaphor for life. As with the greater picture of how we live our lives, we can protect our hearts after a trauma by forming a wall around ourselves, preventing future hurt. The problem with this was that if we guarded ourselves from pain, we also shielded ourselves from experiencing joy.

I thought about my Bill and how he was ripped away from me too soon. Would I betray the memories of Bill if I had had a sexual relationship with Mark? Or was I sheltering my heart from the pain of potential loss? Such questions and their revelations reverberated through my new life in Aix.

La Rotonde at top of Cours Mirabeau

Brussels Sprouts with Lardon

Ingredients

3 slices bacon, chopped, or 1 4 ounce package lardon

1 tablespoon extra-virgin olive oil

1 shallot, chopped

1 1/2 pounds Brussels sprouts, trimmed, small sprouts left whole, larger sprouts halved

Salt and pepper, to your taste

1 cup chicken broth

Brown bacon or lardon in a medium skillet over medium high heat. Remove bacon or lardon to a paper towel-lined plate. Add extra-virgin olive oil to the pan, and add shallots. Sauté 1 to 2 minutes. Add Brussels sprouts, toss and coat in oil. Season with salt and pepper. Cook Brussels sprouts 2 to 3 minutes, until they begin to soften, then add broth. Bring broth to a bubble, cover and reduce heat to medium low. Cook 10 minutes until tender.

Top with cooked bacon or lardon and serve immediately. Serves 4-5 people.

CHAPTER 9

Christmas Present and Christmas Past

Discover Something New Every Day. See With New Eyes.

Christmas present. I had been in Aix for three months and now faced my first Christmas without my family or friends in California. That reality hit me like an avalanche of snow. I felt lonely and depressed. What's more, Mark had departed for London. I was now truly on my own.

I thought of Bill and a Christmas past. He expected his first royalty check from American Management Association for a business book he'd written. When his Parkinson's disease made it difficult for him to leave the house, the idea of having a project together appealed to us. He wrote; I edited.

He wanted to celebrate his writing success and take me to New York for Christmas.

"Of course," I said in a flash. I was so proud of him and his tenacity through all of his physical difficulties, I wouldn't deny him this.

We flew to New York two days before Christmas. Bill and I decorated our room at the hotel festively for the holiday. The following day we spoke of ice-skating at Rockefeller Plaza, something that had long been a dream of my mine.

Bill joined me skating. He seemed to glide effortlessly on the ice. I wished movement was always so easy for him.

Would I ever be as loved and have as beautiful a Christmas again?

Just then the telephone rang, interrupting my memories of Bill.

"*Bonjour et bonne Noel*" It was Vicki Hatton, an Australian friend who was in Paris on business. "What are you doing for Christmas?"

"Nothing," I sulked.

"You must come to Paris. My daughter Natalie and her friend will be here with me. I'd love to have you join us." Vicki was single like me, only several years my junior. We had many things in common— enjoying good food, dressing well, and admiring good-looking men.

"I've missed you," I said. "I'd be thrilled to join you." My self-pitying mood had vanished with Santa Vicki's generous offer.

"Great, come on December 24. We can plan a special Christmas Eve dinner together. We'll shop after you get here. Plan to stay for a few days."

Christmas in Paris! Bill's favorite city all dressed up for the festive season. I could just picture the lights and the displays in the store windows! I gave a prayer of gratitude for Vicki's invitation.

What would I wear? And I needed to bring presents for Santa Vicki, her daughter, and her teenage friend.

I couldn't wait to shop at the Christmas *marché* that spanned the length of the Cours Mirabeau for all the month of December. Little Alpine-style chalets with fake snow on the roofs lined up beside each other, each with a different vendor, offering gifts of all kinds. Handmade candles, purses, scarves, hats, jewelry, sausages, cheeses, candy, and cotton candy. They even offered hot mulled wine. Each shop was decorated for Noel with festive lights and a snowy Christmas tree. The chalet stores were open all day, but it was nightfall that drew out the crowds. That's when the hot mulled wine flowed and children stayed out late to ride on the carousel and partake of the festivities.

Vicki always wore a silver chain with a charm, so I looked for some unusual jewelry that she could wear on her chain. I found a creative jeweler who had made charms from old French coins that were no longer in use. I was drawn to a particular one-franc coin. That would remind Vicki of where we met and of our friendship in Aix. I purchased it and the jeweler beautifully gift-wrapped it for me. On to my next purchase. What would be appropriate for two teenage girls I had never met? Too old for Barbie dolls, yet too young for those fancy condoms that were sold from the French sidewalk vending machines! I laughed as I quickly put that idea out of my mind. I finally chose some dark chocolates shaped like a Christmas tree.

Now I needed to get myself a warm coat, but it had to be chic. I couldn't look like the Michelin Man bulked up against the cold. I could have waited until I got to Paris to buy one, but didn't want to freeze upon my arrival. I entered a store in the *centre ville* and found a beige three-quarter length down coat with a spectacular collar that would show off my multi-colored scarves.

On December 24, I felt like a kid again eagerly awaiting Christmas. I arrived early at the Aix Train Grand Vitesse (TGV) station in time to catch the 8:15 a.m. bullet train. I had pre-purchased my ticket, punched my ticket in the yellow machine that validated it, checked the location of my carriage, and headed down the track to the correct position for easy access to my car. I hopped onto the train, stowed my luggage, and found my seat. No one occupied the seat next to me. Obviously, the French didn't travel on Christmas Eve day. "Thank you, Santa, for my first Christmas present." I took the window seat where I was mesmerized by the landscape whizzing by. Rolling fields and hills dotted the countryside with cows and sheep grazing. I treated the little girl in me with breakfast from the club car. I ordered a *petit déjuener* of baguette, orange juice, and a large coffee. I took it back to my window seat so that I could eat in comfort and enjoy the view.

Upon arriving at Paris-Gare de Lyon, I saw a light mist hovered over the city, very much like Christmas weather should be. I found *Métro* Line Number One to take me to the *Métro* stop, Saint-Paul. Years earlier, I had learned to navigate the Paris *Métro*. I recalled that one needed to know the color or number of the line and to check the final destination to be sure one was going in the right direction. Another challenge was buying tickets from a machine, which had instructions written only in French. Fortunately, today, a woman sat behind the ticket counter. Another Christmas present! Just to be safe, I bought ten tickets from her for future trips while I had the chance.

I got off the *Métro* at Saint-Paul and climbed the never-ending stairs, feeling grateful I had only a small bag to carry. When I reached the top, there stood Santa Vicki Hatton with a welcoming smile.

"*Bonjour*, it is so good to see you." I hugged her and gave her a two-cheek buss.

"So glad you made it," she replied, "Let's go to my apartment. We can celebrate with an *apero*." Vicki was always eager to share a bottle of wine.

We walked the few blocks to her flat, chatting all the way. We had not seen each other for several weeks. Vicki, thin with dark blonde hair, looked as fashionable as ever in her high heels and short black leather jacket.

After a light lunch and some rosé wine, we made plans for dinner. We decided on fresh seafood, cheeses, a baguette, dessert, and wine. Vicki's apartment was in Le Marais, close to Rue Saint-Antoine, a busy shopping street with shops for everything we needed.

We started out at the fishmongers. Vicki wanted fresh oysters. I wanted Dungeness crab. Vicki charmed the fish seller to show us how to open the shellfish with a special knife. He winked and gave it to her as a gift. We left the store with half a dozen fresh, unopened oysters and two cracked crabs. Next, the cheese store where we each picked two favorites; Vicki chose Comté, a sharp, hard cheese, while I chose something soft, Le Délice de Bourgogne. Then to the patisserie for the baguette and a *Bûche de Noël* for dessert on Christmas Day. I selected the one I thought would please the girls, shaped like a log with bright Christmas decorations.

Our shopping almost complete, we were ready for the best part—the wine selection. Vicki knew a spirits store and selected plenty of dry Riesling. With our Christmas Eve dinner ingredients purchased, we headed back to the flat for a rest before the festive evening.

Dinner turned out to be a seafood extravaganza. We spread the shellfish on a platter of cracked ice, then made the remoulade sauce for the crab and the *mignonette* for the oysters. We sliced the baguette while the cheeses warmed up to room temperature. We opened the wine and set the table. Little did we know that opening the oysters would take all of our strength and determination. The fishmonger had opened them so easily that we hadn't noticed his sleight of hand around the shell. We laughed at our clumsy attempts and even tried a hammer on those stubborn shells. They didn't keep us from smacking our lips and sampling the other delights, the crab, bread, cheeses, and the free-flowing chilled wine. Vicki liked oysters more than I did, so she persevered with the little rascals.

After dinner, we took a walk to see the Christmas lights around the Hotel de Ville in Paris, which was the City Hall. Each year, an ice-skating rink was set up for the Christmas season. As we watched the skaters, I imagined with glee Bill gliding effortlessly despite his illness. We moved on to Notre Dame just across the Seine on the Île de la Cité. Mass was being said, so we walked right in and joined them. A choir sang "Silent Night" in French as we found seats. Later, Vicki took communion while I, not being Catholic, waited in my seat. The atmosphere of the dimly lit eight-hundred-fifty-year-old cathedral transported me to the depth of my soul. The scent of burning wax candles created a magical and awe-inspiring experience. I absorbed the energy of all those who preceded us and felt my spirit soar.

Christmas morning arrived and I slept in. When I woke up, I found croissants and *pain au chocolat*. While I was sleeping, Santa Vicki had shopped at the local *boulangerie* for another treat! More delicious French food! More gifts! Only in France are the *boulangeries* open on Christmas.

As Vicki prepared the turkey, I became mystified by the stuffing she purchased. Inside the container there appeared to be brown, plastic clay, which was actually pureed chestnuts, ready to be used as a stuffing for the turkey. Where were the directions? Perhaps I'd led a sheltered life; I'd never seen a chestnut out of the shell, let alone pureed. I thought we should add something like bread, onions, or celery, but in the end we filled the cavity of the bird with the chestnuts and put it into the oven. No roasting chestnuts over an open fire this time.

Vicki set Christmas decorations and candles on the table. I added my Noel Crackers, a British Christmas tradition I had purchased at the Book in Bar bookstore in Aix. I placed one above each individual setting. Then, not knowing when to give my presents, I put one in the center of each plate.

In the foyer, I heard some young voices.

Natalie and her friend Miriam made their first appearance after spending the previous night with a friend. I recognized Vicki's daughter immediately; she had the same look, just younger. Miriam was heavier and had short dark-brown hair and large expressive eyes.

After catching up to date on what they had been doing, we sat down to Christmas dinner in a light-hearted mood. The girls' eyes kept wandering to my wrapped presents on their plate.

"You can open them." They tore into them. Both Natalie and Miriam appreciated the chocolate presents and Vicki was happy with her gift, in memory of our meeting, and immediately put the charm on her chain. We were ready to investigate the crackers. We eagerly snapped our red and green-decorated tube-shaped crackers by pulling the attached string. Each made a resounding *bang!* We read the enclosed fortune for the year. Mine said, "You will soon have a new adventure and meet many new people." We all giggled at the timing of that one. I put on my yellow paper hat, while the girls placed theirs on their heads. Each hat was made in a different color and style. We laughed jovially at the sight.

Then Vicki brought in the beautifully roasted turkey. We all said "Oh-h-h!" The mashed potatoes, gravy, *haricots verts*, and the chestnut stuffing tasted scrumptious. All made a dinner fit for any American or Australian family. We ate until we had Santa Claus stomachs. I brought out the *Bûche de Noël* to more *oohs* and *aahs* from the teens.

After dinner and the dishes, Natalie and Miriam went out with friends while Vicki and I stayed in and watched a DVD, *A Christmas in Paris*.

I had experienced many Christmases — as a child, as a parent with small and grown children, with Bill, and now without Bill. Holidays were always difficult after losing a mate. I missed my two daughters, my son, and my grandchildren. The connection with loved ones was the most important ingredient. I hoped they would be present in my future Christmases.

But this Christmas had turned into a very special one. A new friend was looking out for me, I was in a city that I loved, with festive lights, and I experienced the soul-filled Mass at Notre Dame. Oh so beautiful! I recognized that by being open to a new life, new pleasures had opened to me. What bountiful gifts I received!

A Seafood Extravaganza

Ingredients

Oysters in the shell, number to taste and appetite

Dungeness crab, cooked and cracked. One large crab serves two persons

Prawns, cooked. Number varies according to size and appetite

1/2 cup red wine vinegar

1 tablespoon coarsely ground pepper

2 tablespoons finely chopped shallots

1 1/4 cup mayonnaise

1/4 cup Dijon mustard

1 cup purchased Seafood Cocktail Sauce

Lemon wedges

Sprigs of parsley

Utensils for opening the oysters and crab

Cover a platter large enough for all the seafood with cracked ice. Scrub the shells of the seafood and spread out artistically on the ice.

Meanwhile, mix the pepper, vinegar, and chopped shallots into a *mignonette* for the oysters. Place in a small container to be placed on the platter of ice.

Mix mustard and mayonnaise to make a remoulade for the crab. Place in a small container and place on platter of ice.

Place seafood cocktail sauce for the prawns in a small container and place on platter of ice.

Decorate the platter with the lemon wedges and parsley. Serve immediately with plenty of napkins and finger bowls, if desired.

Serve with a sliced baguette and plenty of wine.

Wendy and Mich celebrate a French New Year's Eve

CHAPTER 10

The Delights of Family

I Sustain Myself with the Love of Family.

Maya Angelou

After saying farewell to Santa Vicki who gifted me with a superb Christmas, I prepared for a visit with my daughter Wendy and son-in-law Mich. They landed in Paris on December 27 from Tucson, Arizona for a five-day visit. Feeling giddy, I headed off on the *Métro* to the hotel near the Eiffel Tower where the kids and I planned to rendezvous.

On my walk from the *Métro* stop to the hotel, I passed a Monoprix, a mini supermarket perfect for gathering the items for a celebratory greeting. First on the list was Wendy's favorite Schramsberg Champagne, then some cheeses, prosciutto, Roget's mini-toasts, marinated olives, cocktail napkins, and a knife to slice the cheese. I assumed that the room would provide glasses. Happy with my selection, I walked to the hotel, anticipating our grand reunion.

In the lobby, I heard a very familiar voice. "*Bonjour, ma Maman.*" I turned to find my older daughter sitting on a chair with a huge smile on her beautiful face. I glowed at the sight of her long blonde hair and her petite figure. She jumped up for a hug. Mich, her handsome husband, beamed at our reunion. Slim and athletic, he greeted me with a kiss.

"*Bonjour, mes chers.*" I squeezed them tightly, then giggled. "Let's see if our rooms are ready, so we can have a real celebration."

The rooms were indeed ready. We headed up and unpacked. I called for an ice bucket, then spread out my delicacies for the welcoming party. After Wendy and Mich had settled in, they banged at my door.

"Come in, welcome to the City of Lights. Tell me about your flight." I wanted to hear everything at once.

Mich popped the Champagne. "Long flight, but nothing unexpected, which is as we like it. Wendy and I are excited to spend five days with you."

Wendy chimed in, "Not to mention we've never been to France before. We want to see where you live."

I beamed. "We can either take the bullet train or drive there."

"Mich wants to drive so we can see the countryside," said Wendy.

"In that case, we need to do an overnight somewhere along the way." After consulting a map, we decided on Beaune, which was halfway to Aix.

The weather outside was cold, rainy and windy, not inviting for exploring the sights of Paris. Nevertheless, we decided to visit the Eiffel Tower, which was in walking distance. We hoped there would be fewer tourists. Perhaps the Champagne had influenced our thinking, because there were as many sightseers as ever who braved the rain. We challenged the line and finally went up the tower. Not surprisingly, the higher we went, the windier it got. However, the view was superb! We could see the Seine River, as well as the Arc de Triomphe in the distance towering over the rooftops.

The weather was friendlier the next day, so we took the Hop-On, Hop-Off bus to allow first-timers Wendy and Mich take in an overview of Paris. It was a two-hour circuit on a double-decker bus. Wanting to get the best view, we headed upstairs for open-air sights. The vistas were clear, but the cold wind was biting. Mich had a red nose while Wendy and I had frozen fingers.

When we reached the Île de la Cité, we hopped off the bus, first to buy knitted hats to keep our heads warm, and then to Notre Dame to light candles for Mich's parents. With this year being the eight-hundred-fiftieth anniversary of the construction of the famous cathedral, many people wanted to visit. We had to endure another long line. This was the only place where Mich patiently stood in line. Fortunately, it moved quickly.

Interestingly, the crowd had been polite but vocal as we waited to enter. However, once inside the cavernous interior, a place of worship for so many people through the ages, voices hushed in awe. The cathedral was dimly lit with the scent of candles and incense wafting in the still air. People ambled slowly in a counter-clockwise direction, taking in the ambience. We joined them circulating around the periphery lined with gated altars representing various saints.

I whispered, "Why do Catholics light candles for people who have passed on?"

Mich explained that saints are invoked by lighting candles. A light shines in the darkness and the smoke lifts the request of remembrance of the soul to the heaven above. He was drawn to the altar of *Saint Anne*, proclaimed as the mother of Mary and grandmother to Jesus. He decided to light two candles, one for each of his parents. Wendy found a different altar, that of Saint Denis, the Patron of Paris, to light a candle. I didn't interrupt their pensive moods to ask what prompted their choices. We continued our silent pilgrimage until we reached the exit.

With nourished souls, we now focused on our bodies.

After finding a cozy bistro for lunch, we ate french onion soup, which warmed our bodies. Then I took them to Île Saint-Louis, which is one of the two islands in the Seine connected with a footbridge, for what else but Bill's favorite stop, Berthillon's, for *une glace*.

I told Wendy and Mich about the first time Bill took me to his best-loved ice cream shop. He wouldn't tell me where we were going. He just indicated it was some-where that had to be seen and experienced. He had all the enthusiasm of a kid being let out of school for the summer. His eyes glistened in anticipation.

I asked Bill "Where were we going?"

He pulled on my hand, hurrying me along the main street of Île Saint-Louis. "I can't tell you, I just want to show you."

After what seemed like a long time, we reached Berthillon, the favorite of Parisians and tourists alike.

His face beamed. "Let's get in line for the best ice cream in the world!"

Bill was a true food-loving Francophile, but loved *glace* more than anyone I know. One day in Italy, he and his grandson Brett (who had the same love), had four helpings of *gelato* before noon.

Bill and I returned many times to Paris and I told Wendy and Mich that it was as if he encouraged me to relive the delightful memory with them. Wendy purchased a dish of chocolate, Mich wanted rum raisin, while I chose a dish of peach ice cream in honor of Bill.

Well nourished, we hopped back on the bus, this time fortified by our warm, knitted caps, and completed the highlights of Paris. When we returned to our original first stop, Wendy and Mich declared they needed to rest as they had a long evening ahead. As birthday presents, I had gifted them a dinner on the well-known *Bateaux Parisiens* Evening Cruise. Nighttime provided a special ambiance on the canal boat that glided along the River Seine for an intimate view of Paris from the water. Bill and I had made the same excursion on our honeymoon in Paris and found it one of our most romantic evenings. I wanted Wendy and Mich to have a similar experience on their special night.

Not wishing to be alone in my hotel room while they were out, I went on my own excursion to the Paris Christmas *marché*. Similar to the Aix Christmas Market, the little chalet stalls were painted white, but with many more lights, making them even more festive.

Even though it was three days after Christmas, shoppers were still out in great numbers. Perhaps they were like me and just wanted to be out and about in Paris. I loved walking, so I worked my way down the *marché* to the Champs-Élysées to view the Christmas lights in that area. I found a welcoming bistro suitable for a woman out alone for dinner. I saved fine dining for occasions with special friends, but didn't mind eating alone in a café, Hemingway style.

The day arrived for our ambitious road trip to Aix. The three of us set out for Le Carousel, the shopping mall that unbelievably was under the Louvre. We picked up a car at the Hertz Rental Agency, and then off we drove south for sunny Provence. At least that's what we thought as we headed out of Paris. But one-way streets, traffic, unfamiliar roundabouts, and general confusion meant one frustrating hour before we were on the fast-moving A6 heading for Beaune.

"Left or right?" asked Mich, our designated driver. None of the signs made sense to us. He panicked. "I could do with some navigation help."

Out of desperation, I called out a response from the back seat. Unfortunately, it didn't take us where we wanted. Mich tried to retrace our tracks, without success. Exasperated, he continued to drive around trying to find our way. When we saw some pedestrians who might help, Wendy rolled down her window. "We're lost," she shouted

They gave directions in French too fast for us to understand. Seeing our blank faces, they repeated their instructions, only louder this time.

Mich sighed. "*Merci.*" As he sped off, he turned to Wendy. "What the hell did they say?"

"Oh, boy," Wendy shouted. "Haven't a clue!"

All of us sat quiet with tension in our bodies. We could have used a helping of Berthillon's now.

Miraculously, we found our way and everyone relaxed. Poor Mich, who was coming down with a cold, left Paris with a poor view of it. Once on the road, his spirits lifted, and we began talking about our favorite memories of Paris.

"The dinner cruise down the Seine was so romantic," Wendy gushed.

"Lighting candles for my parents in Notre Dame, was so special. My parents had often talked about visiting the cathedral," revealed Mich.

"I loved sharing the City of Lights with you two," I said.

Much of the drive was devoted to me telling Wendy and Mich what I knew about Beaune since I had been there twice, the first time with Bill on that cherished honeymoon.

"Bill and I bought a bottle of wine, some cheese, a sausage, and a baguette and found a spot near the river to sit on the grass to picnic. We felt ever so French."

The bed and breakfast in Beaune we saw first was a charming converted chateau. We entered a foyer paneled in dark wood that led to a room filled with French antiques. At the counter, a smiling receptionist greeted us with complimentary glasses of local wine. The price was a little higher than we were used to paying. Mich asked to see a room. When he saw the king-size bed with the fluffy white comforter, he said, "We'll take it," without even consulting us. Not feeling well, he was eager for any bed after the long drive. We checked in quickly. Mich flopped into bed while Wendy and I stretched our legs. We decided to make a tour of the town with the prospect of a little impromptu shopping.

The focal point of Beaune was the original hospice where poor and sick people went to recover or die. Beds lined each side of the main room. Each bed had a view of the chapel with the crucifix in clear view, reminding patients where their healing would come. The roof of the building was covered in a specially designed pattern of bright green, yellow, red, and black tiles made in Spain.

The museum attached to the hospice depicted odd ancient equipment, like a metal contraption for bloodletting—a common practice in those days. Viewing the historical pieces filled me with sadness that so many unnecessary medical procedures went on without helping the patient. Wendy had seen enough and begged to leave.

After our tour of the old hospice, we were ready for some serious window-shopping. Something caught Wendy's eyes.

"Look, Mom, there's a wine tasting in that beautiful old building."

I chuckled. "I think we need to take it in for the sake of investigating an eighteenth-century building."

Thus began our education about the wines of Beaune, here in the heart of the Burgundy Region. We learned that reds were the more popular and well known to

Burgundians, but whites were also now becoming more widespread and reputable.

We started out with three varietals of Chardonnay, but preferred the driest one.

Moving on to three reds, Wendy asked, "How are you really doing, Mom, living here in France by yourself?"

"Thanks for asking. I love exploring France, but Christmas was tough—to be away from family, I really miss Bill right now."

She touched my shoulder. "I'm so glad Mich and I could be with you. We knew this would be a hard time for you, to have a Christmas without Bill."

"Time doesn't always make it easier."

Wendy reached over and squeezed my hand and gave me a loving look with her soft, gentle eyes.

We toasted Bill. I could picture his smile as he raised a glass to me. I clinked his imaginary glass, then returned to wine tasting.

We learned that the Pinot Noir was the most common grape in Beaune.

I told the sommelier, "How about something like a big bold red which I associate with the Burgundy Region?"

With that, he poured their strongest, darkest red. It was dry and bold indeed. We declared it our favorite wine and purchased six bottles to enjoy later in Aix. Feeling very relaxed, we made our way back to our bed and breakfast to find the exhausted Mich sound asleep.

The next morning, Mich still sneezed and coughed on the drive to Aix. Back on the A6, we found the drive more interesting with mountains and pine trees jutting in the countryside. Soon enough, we were in the *centre ville* of my beloved Aix-en-Provence. I was eager to show them the Cours Mirabeau and guide them by the direct route to my apartment. But as often happens in France, something had changed while I was away. A children's ride had taken residence, causing the top of Cours Mirabeau to be closed to traffic. Because I didn't drive in Aix, I didn't know another direct way. After several attempts, I found the way down my narrow one-way Rue Emeric David.

Mich hesitated at the top of the street, looking down the narrow alley. "I don't believe this is possible."

I urged him on. "Cars drive down here all the time."

"Unbelievable," was all he said, when he made it.

At my front door, we left the bags with Wendy in charge. I stayed with Mich to show him the lot where he could park until nightfall, and then had to move the car to another location. Aix was full of parking lots that mysteriously converted to lively restaurants at night, simply by placing tables, chairs, and lighting for diners. By this time, I was sure Mich wondered what I loved about this town of Aix which was doing its best to keep us out. Finally, the car was settled in and so was our ailing Mich. I had given Wendy and Mich the bedroom where I hoped they wouldn't be disturbed by the disco beat until early morning. Thankfully they were spared the *ba boom* from the music downstairs, since the disco was closed. Mich had a good night's rest.

New Year's Eve! We had reservations at Pasino, the local casino for a combination dinner, show, and dancing. Wendy and I chattered in excitement as we dressed in our most elegant clothes. Mich good-naturedly dressed up for the occasion. Three beautiful and handsome people rode in a taxi to the club.

I had asked for a table for three, only to discover we were seated with seven other people. Four of our dinner companions were from Spain and the other three were local Aixois. Wendy spoke both Spanish and French, so she felt exhilarated practicing both languages. Mich and I smiled and struggled along, putting in a word here and there using lots of expressive sign language. For example, I held up three fingers and held my other hand low to indicate I had three children. The dinner was a lovely French four-course meal of baked eggplant appetizer, red pepper and tomato salad, duck breast, and profiteroles for dessert. The show that followed dinner was lost on me with all its French jokes. Wendy and Mich danced and kissed after the midnight toasts, while they each gave me a perfunctory kiss. I felt lonesome without Bill and ready to leave this couples' venue.

Fortunately, they were ready to leave as well, sensing me sitting at the table with strangers, watching them dance as a couple. They were also aware of me having only family to share a midnight kiss.

The next morning, after fresh baguettes and *pain au chocolat* from my neighborhood *boulangerie*, we set out to find the things that charmed me about Aix. The ancient fountains and the seventeenth-century buildings in the Mazarin seduced them, as they had me. Mich was feeling better and seemed to have forgotten the inconvenience of finding parking each day and again at night.

After we spent New Year's Day together, Wendy and Mich had to catch their plane back to the United States.

With a tear in her eyes came Wendy's parting words. "*Au revoir*. Mom, it's so difficult to have you be so far away, but I am so proud of you and what you are doing. You inspire me and so many of my friends."

"Thank you, my dear. I miss you as well. My dream is even better than I imagined. We'll stay in touch with Skype."

They left with an idea of what had charmed their mother away from California, and could better imagine my living a life in France. Over the next several days, I came down from my high with my cherished guests. I felt depressed and experiencing another low, similar to the one I felt before Vicki called, inviting me to share Christmas. A glimmer of doubt plagued my mind that "The Excitement of Discovery," which was my journey this year, might not sustain me. I wanted to banish the feeling.

However, I couldn't help but ponder my desire to live life through non-attachment to things and people. Did I understand it completely? In the moment, I was confused; I had spent three months divesting myself of my personal belongings and prided myself in learning the joy of non-attachment. I had arrived in Aix with three large suitcases, mostly necessary clothing, and did not shop for more belongings. I began to realize that non-attachment to objects and non-attachment to people were two different things. While I had mastered non-possession of things, people were very meaningful to me, especially my family and close friends.

Having Wendy and Mich with me for five days, and seeing them traveling as a couple, had made me miss Bill even more. I was in France experiencing the adventure of a lifetime, but I was doing it alone. Bill's memories were with me, but they were not enough. His physical body was not with me. I decided that what could make this year even more fulfilling would be to have someone with whom to share it.

Instead of dwelling on it, I did what I usually did. *I must get out and do something exciting.*

Duck Breast

Ingredients

2 13-ounce fattened duck breasts

Fleur de sel or fine sea salt and freshly ground black pepper

1 cup hard cider

Heat a heavy skillet over medium heat. When it is hot but not smoking, place the duck breasts in it, skin-side down. Cover and cook them until the skins are deep golden brown, about 8 minutes. Turn the duck breasts and cook them for 2 to 3 minutes on the flesh side, then remove them from the pan. Drain off all of the fat and return the duck breasts to the pan, skin-side down. Continue cooking them, covered, just until the meat is done on the outside, but is still very rare inside, 5 to 6 additional minutes. Remove the duck breasts from the pan and season them with *fleur de sel* and pepper. Add the cider to the pan, scrape up any browned bits from the bottom, and reduce the cider by half, until it is slightly syrupy, about 4 to 5 minutes.

To serve the duck breasts, cut them crosswise on the bias into thin slices and arrange these either on a warmed platter or four warmed plates. Drizzle the slices with the cider sauce and serve immediately.

Makes four servings.

CHAPTER 11

Nicia's Visit

For Every Ending, There's a Beginning

In January, I grappled with the cold weather and my depressed mood provoked by family leaving. Out of the blue, I received a short email from my cousin, Nicia.

Dear Karin

Life is very lonely here for me. I want to get away. May I come to visit you?

Hugs, Nicia

Opposite reactions hit me at once. Yes, I was eager to comfort her; no, she was too fragile for the long flight to France.

Nicia's husband of fifty-nine years had passed away just two months earlier. She was in a critical stage of her bereavement.

I recognized this from the professional experience of leading bereavement groups for over ten years. I also knew firsthand how disoriented and physically nauseated one could feel, especially after losing two husbands. Was she ready to be away from her loving family?

Then I realized that I was part of her loving family, and that she might benefit from my experience. I wanted to provide a respite for her.

I quickly wrote back.

Of course, my dear, you are welcome to come to my home in Aix. Stay as long as you desire.

Lovingly, Karin

Nicia arrived on the first day of February. She was my age, a little taller with short blonde hair. Her drawn, tired face and drooping shoulders demonstrated the huge loss in her life of her husband, Ray, who she met when she was nine and he was ten. They lived on the same street, often had daily contact, and seemed to know each other's thoughts and feelings. They became childhood sweethearts and remained so until his death.

I greeted her with a loving hug at my door. She had endured a long, dreadful flight and had been on a challenging journey since the passing of her beloved Ray.

I dearly loved her and wanted to be helpful during her bereavement and time of adjustment. She told me that my loving presence and guidance were more than enough help. She wanted me to go about my usual activities. And she would let me know if she was unable to participate. So with that directive, we began our time together. Being the good sport, she tried everything, sometimes needing to withdraw to the comfort of her room.

We went to the expat coffee morning at Croquemitoufle and sat around the long table, chatting away. I pointed out to her that she was surrounded by foreigners from Ireland, England, and Holland and, of course, France.

"When was the last time in the United States you had met such diverse people?" I whispered in her ear.

"Are you aware that all of the men are down at your end of the table, surrounding you?" she responded.

I winked. "And you as well."

In the days that followed, Nicia enjoyed our bus trips to nearby villages and tours such as Arles, known for its Roman amphitheater and its famous resident, Van Gogh, the artist who lived and painted over three hundred pictures during his time there. We went to Brasserie Léopold for the Floating Island dessert, which I knew was one of her favorites. We played *petanque* on Sundays, a new activity for her, and we all went for a *pastis apéritif,* mixing the anise-flavored liqueur served with water and ice to our liking.

The first time she washed her clothes, she discovered that after three hours in the combination washer/dryer, the clothes were still wet. In the five months that I had lived there, I never figured out why. I handed her the clothes rack to hang her clothes in the sun, a domestic habit that had become part of my way of life. She was perplexed and overwhelmed by this unusual contraption. Thinking it was all part of her recovery, I didn't offer to help.

Claude, the Canadian gentleman I had met on the bus trip to the Luberon, was wintering in Aix and became part of our lives. We cooked dinners together and went on bus excursions, notably to Chateau La Coste vineyard with a sculpture garden. We spent the afternoon walking the grounds filled with modern art, my favorite a colorful mobile by Joan Miro. I asked Claude, who had also lost a loved one, to help Nicia with some rough steps cut out of stone. I directed them to sit together for a picture. They both agreed to pose for my photograph. Nicia leaned into Claude, as though she wanted to get closer. He looked at her with a sweet smile.

During our month together, she and I spent hours talking about what it was like to lose someone as precious as a husband. We agreed losing a mate meant suddenly your best friend and companion was no longer there to share conversations, visit places, think about, and sleep with. Getting into bed alone was the hardest for both of us. Strangely, we found out that we each slept in one of our husbands' shirts to lessen the pain. Nicia told me she always felt better after we talked.

I slowly witnessed a glimmer of Nicia looking forward instead of back at her loss. Seeing the future without the loved one was vital in the recovery from loss. It usually started in small moments here and there as the genesis to a new way of life. I observed joy creeping back into her face. Worried frowns disappeared.

At the same time, something happened to me. With my concern for her well-being, my spirits lifted. I became more lighthearted and grateful while I comforted my loved one. I realized the importance of relationships in my life. With the budding friendships I was making, in addition to my traveling, *petanque*, and cooking classes, I began to consider extending my sojourn an additional year. My family rebelled, but understood. I had leased my house in California for one year, but that could always be renewed.

I extended my *titre de séjour* (long stay visa) at the local prefecture office. Not surprisingly, it required more documentations and a meeting with French officials. They must have believed I was not a terrorist, because six weeks later I received my extended visa.

Out of the blue, an e-mail arrived that I could not have predicted, from a man who remembered me after a seemingly inconsequential encounter twenty-five years earlier.

I received word from friends in Sedona, Arizona who were so impressed with my upcoming adventure that they wrote about it in a blog to family and friends. A man named Floyd, whom I had briefly met some twenty-five years earlier, had received a copy of the e-newsletter. He had a skiing trip coming up in Europe and wanted to meet up with me, so he asked for my contact information. I remembered the good time we had had at a party at our mutual friends' house long ago. Floyd and I had hung out in the kitchen talking about our lives and bantering about everything and anything. Since that night long ago, we both had lost spouses and were available to kindle a friendship.

Nicia and her favorite Floating Island Dessert.

It had the makings of a romantic story, and I was ready for some romance. Floyd and I e-mailed each other and indulged in late-night phone calls, like teenagers. An avid golfer and skier, he was retired and spent much of his time traveling.

Floyd had the knack of calling at night after I had gone to bed.

"What are you doing?" he asked, when I answered the phone.

I felt like saying, what any sane single woman would be doing—sleeping. Then again, if I had a partner, I wouldn't be sleeping!

Instead, I told him, "Just got into bed, but still awake, what are you doing?"

"I'm looking at my schedule for skiing with my buddies and trying to decide where you and I should meet."

With every phone call, conversations became more intimate.

"I'm at home and wish you were here," he shared.

"Hmm, sounds nice." I wanted to prolong the conversation. "What is your house like?"

"Well, I live on a golf course here in Tustin. I like the serenity of the greens and like being able to walk out after hours to hit a few balls. My house is decorated pretty much with objects from my travels." He then asked, "Are you a cuddler?"

"It depends on where I am and who I am with," came my coy reply.

Floyd and our late-night conversations were all I could think of for weeks. They became an integral part of my discussions with Nicia. The focus became less on her recovery and more on romance. Our talks became a combination of therapy and entertainment for us both. We speculated what it would be like to date someone other than our longtime husbands and what each of us was looking for in a mate.

And did we really want a partner at this stage, or just have a good time dating multiple men?

Before meeting Floyd, I began a regimen of yoga-like exercises, the Five Tibetans, hoping I could flatten my stomach to what it was twenty-five years ago. What a joke after months of eating French food! Nicia and I decided I should have a sexy nightie to wear during the upcoming tryst. Was it wishful thinking that a seventy-eight year old woman could look sexy? France was known for its wide variety of lacy lingerie, so it would surely provide me with the right boudoir attire.

The first ones we saw looked as though they were more fitting for a Barbie Doll figure. Time had changed all that for me. Finally, we saw a lovely ice-blue satin gown trimmed with black lace in a style flattering for my figure and with enough plunging décolletage to titillate a man. Fortunately for my ego, when making the purchase, the sales clerk didn't look at me askance. The prospect of romance overrode age. Oh, the joy!

I later learned from a Frenchwoman friend that it was natural here for a woman to think herself sexy, no matter her age, and to dress the part. This lessened my embarrassment with the saleslady who didn't appear at all shocked. I was doing what many Frenchwomen did. Ooh la la!

In the meantime, Nicia, Claude, and I continued our daily excursions. Sometimes it was just the two of them if I was busy or had little interest in the destination. A special friendship developed between them. Claude seemed an ideal friend to make up for the male presence Nicia had lost.

A door opened for Nicia when she and Claude agreed to stay in contact after both returned to the United States. Apparently, a door was opening for me as well.

All too soon, the five weeks of her visit had passed. Nicia returned home, and I was ready to meet Floyd, my fantasy lover. We had planned to meet in Amsterdam, and as luck would have it, it was the first leg of Nicia's trip home. I booked a ticket on her flight so we could be together a little longer. The hour and three-quarter flight went much too quickly.

My dear cousin, who came to me in such pain, left a more confident person. I was grateful to have played a part in her change as she made her way home alone, to a whole new future. Her life, which had been about raising children and catering to a husband, was now open to creating her lifestyle, exploring who she was, the friends she wanted, and the activities she enjoyed. What a scary and yet exciting time!

I was nervous about meeting Floyd. After all, we had only spent one evening together in the presence of others at a party. But something had clicked that had enabled us to remember each other after all these years.

My eagerness to be in a relationship cast me under a spell of magical thinking that suggested that because this had happened so easily, it must be "meant to be." I knew that he was fun, educated, ambitious, and a world traveler, but I needed to know more. Was he just a player with women? Would this be just a five-day fling or the start of something lasting? I was apprehensive about opening up to another man. I knew too well that the joy of a new relationship also brought the risk of heartache.

Overwhelmed by apprehension and fear, I still felt this was the year of "Excitement and Discovery." I remained open to reinventing myself. That included the prospect of Romance and Love.

Îles Flottantes
Floating Islands Dessert

Ingredients

3 cups milk

1/2 cup plus 1 tablespoon sugar

1 teaspoon pure vanilla extract

4 large eggs, separated

2 teaspoons cornstarch

1 recipe of Caramel Sauce (recipe follows)

In a large saucepan, combine 2 1/2 cups of the milk, 1/2 cup of the sugar, and the vanilla over medium heat and whisk to dissolve the sugar. Bring to a gentle boil.

In a large mixing bowl, beat the egg whites with an electric mixer on medium speed until soft peaks form. Add the remaining 1 tablespoon sugar and continue beating until stiff peaks form. With a wooden spoon, scoop 2 balls of the meringue into the simmering milk mixture. Poach the balls for 2 to 3 minutes, rolling them over with the spoon and basting them with the milk. When all sides are cooked (they are slightly firm to the touch), lift them out with a slotted spoon and set aside on a platter. Scoop 2 more balls from the remaining meringue and repeat the process. The meringues can be stored for about 1 hour, loosely covered with plastic wrap, in the refrigerator until ready to use.

In a small mixing bowl, combine the remaining 1/2 cup milk, the egg yolks, and cornstarch and whisk together. Slowly whisk 1/2 cup of the warm milk mixture that the meringues were cooked in into the egg mixture, then pour back into the remaining warm milk in the saucepan. Whisking constantly, bring the mixture to a gentle boil and cook until it thickens enough to coat the back of a wooden spoon, about 2 minutes. Remove from the heat, pour into a glass bowl and let cool to room temperature. Cover with plastic wrap, pressing the wrap down against the surface of the custard to keep a skin from forming. Refrigerate for at least 4 hours or up to 8 hours.

To serve, gently stir the custard, then spoon equal amounts into four dessert bowls. Set a meringue ball on top of each and drizzle with the caramel sauce.

Caramel Sauce

Ingredients

1 cup sugar
1/2 cup water
1 cup heavy cream

In a small, heavy saucepan, combine the sugar and water and bring to a boil, stirring often. Cook, stirring occasionally, until the mixture is a deep caramel color and has the consistency of a thick syrup, 10 to 15 minutes. Remove from the heat. Stir in the cream, return the saucepan to high heat and boil the sauce until it is the consistency of a thick syrup, about 2 minutes. Let cool. The sauce can be refrigerated until ready to use. Allow it to reach room temperature before using it. Yields about 3/4 cup.

CHAPTER 12

The Elephant in the Hotel Room

Take risks and create adventures

ℐ *arrived an hour early* at Schiphol, the Amsterdam airport, anxious to greet Floyd. My flight from Marseilles landed before his, so I spent the time at the arrival gate, outside customs and the baggage claim, watching people and nervously fidgeting with my suitcase. It carried my blue satin nightgown. I hoped I'd get to wear it.

I was always amazed how different in appearance people seemed in the various airports I had travelled. After an hour of observing passengers, I found the Dutch to be tall with blond hair, blue eyes, and ruddy cheeks. Then I wondered what they had in their suitcases — perhaps red nightgowns.

In early March, the temperature outside was 3° Celsius, or 36° Fahrenheit. Early in my stay in France, I had learned to quickly convert from Celsius to Fahrenheit by doubling the number and adding thirty.

Passengers were dressed in hats, scarves, gloves, warm coats, and boots. It struck me that I was a long way from my native home in Southern California, where even the winter months were temperate.

When I hadn't received any messages after my plane landed, I became troubled. Floyd and I depended on making contact via our smartphones to locate each other. To ease my concern, I found two young men who were promoting cell phones. I told them about my need to find Floyd. They immediately checked my cell phone and changed my settings to roaming while in the Netherlands. I thanked them and thought to myself it must be wonderful to be so knowledge-able about the virtual world. Young people seemed to have little fear of anything technical and an ability to fix anything.

Sitting in the arrivals section, waiting for Floyd to leave the plane, I felt like a teenager full of excitement. *What will he be like? Will he like my satin nightgown?*

I searched the faces of everyone coming through the arrivals door. Were they too looking for someone? The only identifiable feature I remembered of Floyd was that he was tall and athletic. Three-fourths of the men who appeared fit that description. I kept watching intently for the next hour, creating one reason or another in my mind why he wasn't there. The computer screen showed that the plane had landed. Perhaps his luggage was delayed, or he was at another door. The questions went on for an hour and a half. My stomach knotted into a ball. *Where the heck is he?* Was I being stood up all this way from France?

Just at that moment, a nimble figure jumped in front of me and planted an energetic three-cheek kiss on my face.

Startled, I asked, "Floyd?" I hid my annoyance and relief.

"And I know you are Karin from your beautiful face and blond hair," he replied, scrutinizing me with an odd look in his eyes.

I gazed at his wrinkled face and bald head and slumped in disappointment. I read his dismay as well. We both had aged. Had we not expected that? After all, twenty-five years had passed. I was surprised at my reaction. I could leave Southern California, but I couldn't take that youth-centered belief out of my mind. After pondering the wasted seventy-six euros on my beautiful nightgown, I noted with some reassurance that Floyd had lots of energy, great posture, and a positive attitude.

"Let's get out of here and head into Amsterdam," said Floyd, showing his alpha male side. "There is a train here at the airport which will take us to Central Station. From there we can take a tram to our hotel."

"Sounds good to me." I glanced at my watch. "I've sat here long enough." Happy to get moving, I gathered my things.

"Sorry about the wait. Had some shopping to do in the airport mall," Floyd said casually.

Shopping? What am I, chopped liver? And where are my flowers!

Floyd led us the short distance to the train, going up the stairs the wrong way first, then retracing the steps to get to the right side of the tracks where the train was going into Amsterdam. I felt like we were walking in circles. His navigational skills seemed faulty.

The train journey to Central Station passed quickly. As we got off to board a tram that would bring us close to our hotel, I was stunned by the thousands of bicycles in the street. Never had I seen so many in one place.

"Welcome to Amsterdam," said Floyd. He rubbed his stomach. "I'm famished. We should get a bite to eat at a restaurant I know." He didn't wait for my answer.

I was hungry and I wanted to postpone our arrival at the hotel a little longer. I needed a little more time before broaching the subject of the sleeping arrangements.

In the restaurant, Floyd was clearly well known. The waitstaff referred to him by name and showed us into a room with a fireplace, which was cozy on such a frigid day. I wondered about his history in this café, since everyone recognized him. Not only did my bones need warming up, but my disappointment needed thawing out as well.

We ordered fondue. Floyd had a beer and I a glass of red wine. The fondue arrived steaming hot in two bowls, filling the air with a rich gruyère cheese aroma. As Floyd talked about the success of his ski trip, I half-listened while trying to figure out the reason for my confusion. The cheerful laughter that we'd had on the phone over the last two weeks was conspicuously absent.

"Did you really remember me from the party at Steve and Meg's?" I asked, moving the conversation to something more personal.

He dipped a cube of bread into the cheese. "Absolutely! Having way too much fun for two married people, even though we were in the open kitchen in full view of the other partygoers."

That was exactly how I remembered the day. I also thought at the time that I wished my husband Bill had been more spontaneous. Bill had a great sense of humor, but it didn't come off in social situations, unless he knew the people well. How could I have been so critical of him?

We finished lunch and set off for the moment of truth. Floyd became confused within a few blocks of the hotel. He thought it was in a certain direction so we headed off on foot. Because his head was shaved, he complained it was getting numb from the cold air. He stopped abruptly in front of a shop with knitted caps. He went in and bought a Dutch hat with the braids hanging down on each side to cover the ears. He thought I should buy one too. I didn't want to look as silly as a man with flapping braids. Maybe I didn't need the satin nightgown after all! But we were both happy that his head was now warm.

We carried our luggage and walked in circles. We were lost. Floyd spied an office for the Rijksmuseum We ducked in to get out of the cold and asked for help. The kind office receptionist couldn't give directions, but she offered to let me stay in the warm building while Floyd continued his search. She showed me to a chair and gave me a cup of coffee. About half an hour later, Floyd returned with a map, a refreshed sense of direction, and a look of pure delight on his cheery face. He triumphantly guided me the short five blocks to the hotel.

The small European boutique hotel was cozy and charming, two aspects I appreciated immensely. At the desk, they looked at his I.D. "Mr. and Mrs. Anderson? A standard room?"

"That would be fine," Floyd said, not bothering to correct the mistake.

As we headed up to the room, I was amazed at how passive I'd become. Perhaps I was in shock that I was with a man I didn't know, who lost his direction, and wore a ridiculous hat.

"The room will be small but adequate," Floyd warned me.

Adequate for what? I wondered. *Does the room have one bed or two?*

We opened the door. Two single beds stared at me from opposite sides of a cramped room. I felt relief and disappointment, both at once!

"I chose to be on the safe side when reserving the room," Floyd answered.

I dropped my suitcase. "Thank you. That was very sensitive of you." I replied.

"I'm not always insensitive, Karin."

Only when you stranded me at the airport while you shopped.

He unpacked his things into a drawer. "What do you want to do while we are here?"

I glanced at my suitcase.

"The Rijksmuseum is closed for renovation, but there are others."

Mr. Romance he is not. I suggested, "The Anne Frank Museum, the Van Gogh Museum, and the Flower Market are at the top of my list."

He smirked, "What, no trip to the Red Light District?" *Huh?* "Well, if you insist." I smiled.

We went downstairs for an aperitif and spent what was left of the afternoon talking and getting to know each other. After Floyd's wife died of a heart attack, he was devastated emotionally and married on the rebound to a younger, beautiful woman. They had several years of an unhappy marriage, had two children together, and were now in the process of a divorce. He admittedly was in an unstable place and time in his life. In turn, I brought him up to date with what had been going on in my life, the emotional drain of Bill's illness, his death, my retirement, and now my new life with a move to France. The hours flew by until it was time for dinner.

After our meal, we took in the Red Light District via a tuk tuk, a bicycle with a seat behind the peddler. We jumped on and got under the blanket in the near-freezing night air. Our driver took us around the area and then suddenly stopped, saying he couldn't go any deeper into the District where it was forbidden. We got out and strolled in the bitter cold. My teeth chattered. In the windows, women dressed in lacy bras and panties beckoned to us to come in. Some even put up three fingers indicating they would like both of us to come in for a little three-way action. Some smiled with a friendly, come-hither look; others looked sultry and bored as if they wanted someone to please them. They all moved their bodies in suggestive, enticing ways. If the curtains were open and they were in full view, they were available. If the drapes were closed, they were occupied, satisfying customers.

An Amsterdam style parking lot

This business was fully accepted in Amsterdam. I felt sad that these women put their bodies on display. I could only imagine what they went through to earn a living. I didn't feel the same way about the men, drag queens who were beautifully made up with long flowing hair, clean-shaven, and open silk robes that revealed sequined bustiers complete with cleavage. Easily mistaken for women, the drag queens looked like they were costumed for a theatrical production. They strutted with an air of pride.

As we moved from window to window, my fingers in my coat pockets were becoming blue, and face and nose frozen numb. I could not go on much longer. Since we had no intention of becoming customers, we headed back to our hotel. We hadn't taken a card from the hotel with the address to give to a taxi driver, so we boarded a tram. We got off at the wrong stop and became lost, yet again. Even I, who normally had a good sense of direction, became disoriented. We walked briskly in one direction for a while with the freezing wind at our backs, then decided to change course. After half an hour, I was chilled to the bone.

"I'm too cold to go on." I spied a pub that was open and barged in. "You find the hotel and come back to get me. Take a taxi if you need to."

"Okay," Floyd said. He stumbled out in the cold while I sat with an Irish Coffee in the heated pub.

Floyd was an intelligent man and a world traveler, but something was amiss. Was he avoiding being in the hotel room with me without wanting to say it? Did he have another lover? Or was he getting confused in his latter years?

He returned looking pleased with himself. He found the hotel. I finished my coffee and soon was safe in the warmth of the room. No nightgown that night!

The next day we were ready for a full day of adventure. Floyd gave me a map. "Can you read this?"

"I use maps on all my travels. I'll get us to the Anne Frank Museum."

Strolling along the boat- and tree-lined canals, we gazed at the tall narrow houses. Floyd explained that they were built that way for tax purposes. They were taxed on how wide they were.

He grabbed my arm when I was about to walk into the path of a bicycle. "You must know that cyclists have the right of way here. They don't stop for pedestrians. They even have their own lanes, signs, and signals."

"I have never seen so many bicycles in one place. I suppose it is an economic thing."

"Space is limited and parking is very expensive, not to mention fuel."

Following the map, I guided us to our destination. Fortunately, the line was very short at the Anne Frank Museum so we queued up. The museum narrated the story of the thirteen-year-old Jewish girl. I was moved to tears, being in the house of Anne and her family hiding in the attic to avoid being sent to a concentration camp. I couldn't help thinking of my own children at that age, wondering how they would have coped.

Still pondering the tragic life of Anne Frank, I needed a more comforting site for our next stop. The Flower Market consisted of individual shops lining several blocks along a musty-smelling canal. There were few flowers due to the cold weather, but many bulbs, seed packets, garden ornaments, plants for sale, and artificial flowers providing color. I imagined how full of life and fragrant aromas it would be in the spring with tulips, hydrangeas, cyclamen, and hyacinths. I bought a packet of tulip bulbs to plant when I returned to France.

I felt hope that while I was standing in this latent garden, in a few months it would be bursting with blossoms. I couldn't help but wonder if my love life might be blooming as well.

Floyd and I spent five days together. During that time, we had fun and kind moments. Over dinner on two different nights, he introduced me to three of his friends in Amsterdam. He always pulled off my boots when I returned to the hotel. At a grocery store, he bought orange tulips for our room, arranging them into two bouquets, putting one in the bedroom and the other in the bathroom. One day he asked me if I'd like to feel his bald head. It had a rather sensuous feel to it, but nothing developed from my obvious delight in stroking his bare skin. Another day, he asked if I'd like to shave his head, I declined, as I feared nicking him. Finally, he proudly showed me what he had purchased at the airport mall. It was a small appliance to trim the hairs from his nostrils!

I had been stood up at the airport for a nose trimmer?

Just the thing Mark, the retired literature professor who had been my friend before he returned to England, needed on those cold nights in Aix when his nose dripped down his hairs. Where was it then!

Floyd even took me to an Indonesian dinner that consisted of over fifty dishes. We sat at a doublewide table to accommodate the small dishes filled with rice, beef, chicken, fish, egg, and vegetables of various kinds until fifty bowls surrounded us. Amazing and delicious!

Though we were together five days, I never got a sense of what was going on between us. I chose not to ask him directly. Was I worried about being rejected? Was I frightened of the truth? Was it the pain of his divorce, was he in another relationship, was my age truly a turn-off to him? Was I so disappointed that the relationship I had had such high hopes for wasn't materializing as I imagined, that I was not able to keep up my end of the mischievous repartee? Somehow when we were face to face, there was no chemistry between us.

This one will do.

Toward the end of our time together, I finally asked him. "Floyd, why did you want to meet me over here in Europe?"

He shrugged his shoulders, but didn't face me. "I like meeting and knowing people all over the world. You've seen how many friends I have here in Holland. Besides, I trusted our friends in Arizona. They said you were incredible."

Floyd never told me I was incredible. Maybe he collected people all over the world, and I was part of his people connection. I didn't pursue the question further. I found it strange that from the magical beginning we shared at a distance, that we had so little attraction to each other on sight.

Maybe spontaneity and excitement weren't all they were cracked up to be. My thoughts turned to Bill and his shyness, and how he held his quick wit in reserve for those he knew well. I now appreciated that quality so much more. I realized there were moments between people that were full of intrigue, but the connections that last a lifetime were rare indeed.

On our last day, I packed my suitcase for my return to France, carefully placing the unwrapped blue satin nightgown in its fragile tissue paper underneath my clothes. Still in pristine condition, it waited for a more appropriate special occasion, or so I promised myself.

"Thank you, Floyd, for showing me Holland." I gave him a little hug.

He embraced me. "It was a pleasure. It's what I do best. I do hope you will welcome me when I visit you in Aix. You can be my tour guide."

"Yes, of course," I said, not sure I really meant it.

At the airport, I shook my head in wonder. After my years of counseling clients to be upfront with their feelings, I had spent five days in a bedroom with a man, dancing around an elephant. However, Floyd opened me to the idea that my year of excitement could include love.

Maybe I hadn't wasted seventy-six euros on that blue satin nightgown!

Cheese Fondue

Ingredients

8 ounces Gruyère cheese, cut into ¼-inch cubes

4 ounces aged Emmental cheese, cut into ¼-inch cubes

2 tablespoons all-purpose flour

1/8 teaspoon cayenne pepper

1/4 teaspoon freshly ground white pepper

1 1/3 cups medium-bodied white wine

1 tablespoon kirsch (cherry brandy)

2 teaspoons freshly squeezed lemon juice

Sourdough bread, cut into 1-inch cubes

Assorted vegetable, cut into pieces, for serving

1 stand and 1 Sterno can

Toss cheeses in a medium bowl with flour, cayenne pepper, and white pepper to coat, and set aside. Heat wine in a fondue pot over medium-low heat until it starts to bubble, about 5 minutes.

Stir in cheese mixture, a little at a time. Stir in kirsch. Continue to cook, stirring, until cheese has melted, up to 20 minutes. Stir in lemon juice. The mixture should be smooth and almost bubbling.

Transfer pot to its stand set over a burner. Serve immediately with bread and vegetables.

Spring and Jan arrive in Aix

CHAPTER 13

Jan Arrives

Life Moves On

Hope To see you while I am in Aix. Will be there from April 2 until the 9th.

Jan's email arrived the last week of March. I flashed back to five months earlier when Jan and I had attended the French class together at one of the Aix language schools.

When in class, I had noticed him sitting across the room, small in stature with short gray hair, wearing a muted gray plaid shirt and a two-day-old stubble on his chin. He was the only man in class close to my age. However, his serious, almost dour demeanor marked him as someone I wasn't particularly interested in befriending. Then, unexpectedly, Jan approached me during the coffee break.

Waiting to order coffee, he turned to me. "I am going to Marseille by bus this afternoon after class. Would you like to join me?"

"I was planning to go shopping for groceries, but that could wait. I haven't ventured out of town, so I would love to see more of the country."

"We should meet at the Gare Routière at 1:30 to catch the bus," he instructed. He then ordered coffee for both of us.

At the appointed time, we met at the bus stop for Marseille, bought our tickets, and settled in for the twenty-minute trip. Jan had visited the area many times before, and sat by the window as we rode along.

He pointed out the TGV (Bullet Train) station as we passed, and how that particular train took only two and one-half hours to get to Paris. I noted how the arid terrain was similar to parts of Southern California.

"What brought you from Holland to Aix?"

Jan paused before speaking. "I love Provence and wish I could live here all the time. First I need to know the language." He had spent two weeks visiting Aix.

"Is it just the language that keeps you from coming now?" I asked.

"Actually, I have a ninety-four-year-old mother who needs my attention."

His caring touched me. "I came to France partly to learn the language," I said. "We seem to have the same desires."

The conversation flowed easily and very soon we were nearing our destination. I could see that we were coming to the outskirts of Marseille as apartment buildings, factories, and graffiti appeared in view. Very much like the outskirts of any large city.

Gare de Marseille-Saint-Charles, the bus and train station in Marseille, was a combination of very old and very new construction.

Jan tugged at my arm. "Follow me. I want to show you something."

When we got outside the building, I was stunned by the beauty of the Beaux Arts staircase that led down to the city. It was appropriately named *Le Grand Escalier* and was built in the late nineteenth century during the Belle Époque era. Lovely marble statues of naked women, a wrought iron bannister, and ornate lampposts set off the grandeur of the wide marble steps. Some people were sitting on the steps enjoying the loveliness of the scene. I asked Jan to take my picture to immortalize the scene. He obliged, and we then set off to the Old Port, ten minutes away.

At the harbor, Jan told me he felt right at home near the water because he once owned a boat in Holland. He pointed out a thirty-five-foot powerboat similar to his. We continued walking past the harbor, up a hill to the Palais du Pharo where we found a bench on the spacious green lawn to rest and people-watch.

He furrowed his brow. "It is the six-month anniversary of my wife's death. I didn't want to be alone." He smiled at me, "I am so glad you could come today."

He told me she had been a hard worker, but very depressed. She found life too difficult and, in the end, took her own life. His eyes watered as he told me the tragic story of discovering her lovely body hanging in their bedroom. No wonder he always looked depressed to me. It had actually been the pain of heartache. I reminded myself to be more understanding and to not be so quick to judge others.

I thought I had learned the lesson of being judgmental years ago when Bill and I went out to eat. My habit was to silently judge young men if they wore tank tops and baseball caps in restaurants. At one point during the meal on a particular evening, Bill's medication began to wear off and he had a hard time standing. Two of those sloppily dressed young men generously helped Bill stand up. They became my new best friends. With their strong arms, they easily had him on his feet and ready to move. That memory filled me with emotion. I had prejudged Jan like I had the two young men.

Jan's vulnerability encouraged me to open up. I understood the pain he was feeling. I shared some stories about my husband's death. We talked about how difficult it was to lose a mate. Not only the sorrow of it, but starting life all over again.

Before I moved to Aix, I thought I would be getting away from death and the cares of my counseling practice. But now I saw how death was part of life. It was everywhere. I was grateful to be with Jan on his emotional anniversary day.

We returned to the port and had an *apero* before heading to the bus station. On the way, he took my arm as we moved through the crowded streets. I felt comforted and protected to have a man watching out for me.

"Do you date in Holland?" I asked casually.

"I can't even think of being with a woman other than my wife."

"You will at some point. Don't feel guilty about it," came my words of wisdom.

On the bus ride back to Aix, we talked of other things. Jan began to speak about gardening in his yard. His favorite time of the year was spring, when he could be planting vegetables and flowers to share with his mother.

When I saw him again the next day at school, the teacher instructed us to practice our French by telling the class what we had done the previous afternoon. When it was Jan's turn, he said, "*Mon amie et moi avons pris en bus à Marseille.*" (My friend and I went by bus to Marseilles.)

Oh, good, I thought, *he considers me his friend.*

After class, I drummed up the courage to ask him to my apartment for lunch the following day, in exchange for him hanging a trellis on my patio. Since he liked gardening, surely he would know how to do that. I was still learning what was acceptable behavior in this foreign country without appearing too suggestive. In addition to the cultural differences, I wondered if I, as a single woman, could invite a man to my apartment without implying something sexual.

He arrived promptly. I offered him a glass of rosé while I showed him my patio with the unhung trellis. I served strawberry chicken salad for lunch. While we ate, Jan discussed his plans for returning to Holland at the weekend. He hung the trellis efficiently and quickly, then prepared to leave.

"We are good friends," he said, and gave me a hug and the Dutch three-cheek kiss.

What does "good friends" really mean?

When he returned to Holland, and kept in contact by email, first in French to practice what we had learned in class, and then he switched to English. I followed suit.

Six months had passed since that trellis-hanging lunch. I reread part of his email. *Hope to see you while I am in Aix.* I hoped he was ready to start dating. We were good friends, after all. That should count for something. I remembered the emotions we shared while comparing the similarities of what we had been through. I fantasized about a deeper connection leading to romance while he was in town. I was ready. Would the nightgown come out of its tissue?

Jan phoned me the next day. Because of the fiasco with Floyd, I was keen to see him.

I trembled with excitement as I held the phone, "It has been so long since you left for Holland."

"The weather was so cold last winter," he said.

"I'm eager to hear how things are going for you," I said. "You were pretty sad when you left. I enjoyed your mail and wanted to tell you I missed you."

I hoped he got the message without my being too forward.

There was a long pause before he replied. "I feel better," he said. "My girlfriend is traveling with me."

Karin's Strawberry Chicken Salad

Ingredients

One head romaine lettuce

One chicken breast, cooked

One basket fresh strawberries

One cup shredded mild cheese

1/2 cup toasted slivered almonds

1/4 cup white balsamic vinegar

2 tablespoons virgin olive oil

Into a large salad bowl, tear lettuce into bite-size pieces. Chop chicken breast into cubes. Clean and slice strawberries. Put all ingredients into the salad bowl and toss. Make a vinaigrette from the vinegar and oil and toss into salad.

Serve immediately with sliced crusty baguette and a chilled rosé wine. Serves 2.

Ready for Guiness with Liam. He's a bit bashful.

CHAPTER 14

My Little Leprechaun

*Be Open to Romance; You Never Know
What Will Happen*

The shock of Jan having a girlfriend jolted me to reflect on the months I'd been in France. I realized I had been eager to be in a relationship shortly after arriving. I yearned for connection, for touch, and affection. Just as infants need touch and affection to thrive, so do I, or for that matter, so does any human being. I wanted to be touched to feel loved and nurtured.

Fortunately, my dear friends Gaby and Michael visited me in the summer. They helped rectify the problem. I had worked with Gaby at a preschool for visually impaired children twenty years ago. A small Indonesian woman with dark hair and beautiful skin, Gaby was the metaphysical one, whereas Michael, tall and blond, was the fixer. Michael worked with me as a counselor in a bereavement group.

I welcomed my dear friends like family here in Provence. After plentiful hugs, I said, "I can't wait to show you the lavender fields."

"I also want to taste the bouillabaisse in Marseille," said Gaby.

"They're famous for the fish soup," I agreed.

Gaby smacked her lips. "Can't wait." She then winked. "By the way, do you have a special man in your life, Karin?"

I told her and Michael of my brief encounters with Floyd and Jan and sighed about the unworn blue satin nightgown.

The Indonesian woman peered in my eyes as if looking into crystal balls. "Your lack of a relationship is an astrological issue," she said. "You are not meant to be in a relationship until the new year."

"I don't believe that for a minute," huffed Michael, ready to fix the problem. "Are you registered on a French dating site?"

I blushed. "No, I haven't felt secure enough here to venture out there."

"Well, we're going to fix you up while we are here!" With that, Michael opened his iPad and searched for matchmaking sites.

During the rest of the afternoon, Michael helped me complete my profile and snapped a new picture of me on the terrace. He then uploaded the image which flaunted my hostess skills as well as my supposed appeal. I felt like a teenager again.

While my mind was contemplating Mr. Right, Michael attended to the next problem — where to find the best bouillabaisse. They wanted something elegant, like Chez Fou Fou. Searching for the right restaurant was just as difficult as finding Mr. Right. As it turned out, the restaurants were either closed or booked out. I hoped I would have better luck with a man.

When I took Michael and Gaby to the airport, Gaby laughed about the trip to Marseille; she named it "The Great Bouillabaisse Caper."

Michael hugged me and said, "Good luck with the Internet dating."

Several weeks passed without a response. But then I received one from a fifty-four-year-old man in Switzerland. This seemed like a bit of a stretch, both age- and location-wise, but my inquisitiveness got the best of me.

"Did you notice my age?"

"Oh, age is no problem. I am willing to move," answered the younger man's email. "You are so beautiful."

I dubbed him, "The Great Sugar Mama caper." I didn't respond.

I ignored a few others until I heard from Liam, Irish for Bill. The seventy-one-year-old retired Christian Brother lived in Ireland. *Jesus, Mary and Joseph!* I never thought of going out with a monk!

Not being Catholic, I thought priests and brothers usually were married to God for a lifetime, but they had an excellent education—a priority for me—and he was within my age range.

Where do you live? he wrote in an email.

I typed on my computer. *Aix-en-Provence. I spent several weeks in Shannon, Ireland, and I enjoyed the pubs and friendly people. I thought Brothers weren't supposed to have girlfriends.*

I wanted to establish some credibility. No Irish blarney for me.

He replied, *Dear Karin, Being celibate would be a requirement if I was still working, but I am retired. I had a lady friend in London for several years, but she passed away last year. I am very lonely.*

That made two of us.

The emails continued. Eventually we decided to Skype. I enjoyed seeing his white hair and handsome face. Sometimes I could hardly understand what he was saying due to his thick Irish accent, but I always understood the twinkle in his eye.

When he asked about me and my activities, I felt that he cared. We talked about what we were reading and the movies we had seen. Soon we made plans to meet. For some reason, trying to connect from Newtown, where Liam lived, to Aix would take twelve hours, because there were no direct flights. That made it almost as long as it took to get to Los Angeles, so we started thinking of other places to meet. London seemed the logical choice. I would go via the low-cost airline RyanAir to Stansted, an airport outside London. We would meet there and then travel into London the next day.

On the day of our meeting, Liam landed before I did and waited outside the arrival door at Stansted Airport. I recognized him right away. He looked very Irish in his plaid cap with wisps of white hair showing.

The scent of his hat smelled like real Irish wool; however, I detected alcohol on his breath. He walked with a cane as he came to greet me. I was shocked that I almost towered over the five-foot man, even though his profile had claimed he was a full five feet six inches. We all shrink a little with age, but Liam lost six inches! I wondered if anything else had shrunk. In my mind, I nicknamed him My Little Leprechaun.

In the late afternoon, we headed over to the hotel at the airport where Liam had reserved two rooms. After unpacking, we met in the lounge bar where we found ourselves two comfy chairs in the slightly darkened room.

"What will ye be takin', Ca' rinn?"

"A French rosé, thank you."

He smiled. "Lovely choice for a lady."

He ordered a Guinness and a double shot of Jameson Irish whiskey.

"You mentioned on Skype that you stayed in Florida. Where?" I asked.

"Oh ay! I got sent to the foreign missions, Miami. I was a Christian Brother, part of a Catholic order of men who teach school. The people were very different there, all walks of life, as the fellas say in the pub! It was mighty hot, oh, far different than where I was reared."

"Did you like being a Brother?"

"Indeed I did. I had little demands, unlike the head person, his Lordship the bishop. Now be tellin' me about ye."

I sipped my wine. "Well, as you know, I married my childhood sweetheart at a very young age and had three children. I went back to school after they were in school and haven't stopped learning since."

The conversation flowed through the evening. I felt relaxed with My Little Leprechaun. His eyes twinkled when he talked. He had worked with people enough to understand emotions and be concerned with them. He was also a good listener, something I always looked for when meeting someone. I liked finding out how spiritual someone was. In Liam's case, I discovered later that being religious was not the same as being spiritual.

Before retiring to my own room for the night, I gave Liam a French two-cheek kiss goodnight.

I put on my pajamas and settled into my room.

Brring, brring. I picked up the telephone. "Hello?"

"Ca' rinn, would ye be ever so kind as to come to my room and help me figure out how the shower goes?"

He wanted me to work his shower? What the heck was he talking about? I had to see what he wanted.

At his door, he greeted me with a passionate kiss.

He doesn't want help with the shower; he wants help with his plumbing tool! I quickly showed him the mechanics of the shower and hurried back to my room. After all, I had my three-date rule to uphold. No sex until the third date, and the man definitely had to shower!

We met for breakfast the next morning and then headed to London, first by Underground to Liverpool Street Station, and then by a red double-decker bus to the Kensington area.

"Ca'rinn, would ye be comfortable with just one sleeping room at the hotel?"

Taken a little aback, I remembered my blue satin night-gown I packed, just in case. "Well, I need to let you know that I snore," I said. "That could be a problem for you."

"That won't be a problem. I have me earplugs in me bag."

I was surprised to hear myself say, "Okay, but we need two beds."

Liam winked. "That suits me."

After several hours of traveling, we arrived at our Kensington stop. Liam spotted The Goat, the oldest pub in London. He'd never walked so fast!

He guided me there. "Are you fine with pulling in for a lovely dinner?"

"Dinner?"

Liam explained. "It's me dinner time now, but I know ye don't take yours 'til me supper time. I don't like eating much before bed. And The Goat is very grand, I hear."

We went into the darkened interior and found a pol-ished wooden bar up front with several golden levers that poured tap beer and ale. Off to one side were tables for customers to order a meal or drinks. We found a table in the front, close to the bay window and checked the menu.

"I'm going to try a shepherd's pie and a Guinness," I said to the waitress. Liam ordered a sandwich and fries, along with a Guinness and a double shot of Jameson.

The shepherd's pie, a traditional British fare, arrived steaming hot, wafting odors of beef, carrots, and pota-toes. I was famished; the tasty food disappeared quickly. Liam and I lingered, savoring our ales.

"We are very close to Kensington Palace where Kate and William live," he said, before ordering another Guinness.

"Can we visit the duke and duchess?"

"Only the grounds, but they are beautiful, I am told."

We finished our drinks around two p.m. and walked to the hotel. Liam shuffled slowly due to an arthritic knee. His cane provided stability. I found the crawling pace awkward but slowed down, not wanting to get ahead of him.

At the hotel, a large fresh flower arrangement greeted us in the lobby, fragrant and beautiful. That first impression upon arrival has always been my way of appraising a restaurant or hotel. Tall, yellow Spanish Broom surrounded by shorter stems of tulips, stargazer lilies, and hydrangeas in shades of beige and white filled a large silver vase resting on a circular, dark wood table. Soft, elegant music added to the welcoming atmosphere. This upscale hotel made me feel like a duchess.

Our room, spacious for an inner city hotel, had been decorated in restful shades of blue and turquoise. A modern headboard of blond wood, stretching across the space between the two beds, dominated the room. The large, fluffy pillows on the bed were immediately inviting. His and her robes hung in the closet with little terry scuffs for our feet sat on the closet floor. I felt so welcomed in this cozy hotel room.

"How about taking the Hop-On, Hop-Off bus for a tour of London this afternoon?" I asked.

"That sounds lovely to me. When were ye thinking on going, Ca'rinn?" He glanced at the bed.

I disregarded his invitation and asked, "Why not now?"

Off we went to a bus stop close to the hotel. The circuit took two hours and passed many of the main attractions of London. I made a note to come back to the National Gallery the next day.

As we approached St. Patrick's Church, Liam said he knew the Bishop. I asked if he would introduce me to him. Liam initially hesitated but agreed. So we got off the bus.

We entered the silent, darkened sanctuary and spoke in hushed voices. We passed by several altars scattered around the perimeter of the church. Liam led me out through a side door to an offices area. Liam knocked on one of the doors.

A voice answered, "Come in."

When we entered, a tall, thin man, dressed in a purple cassock with a large cross dangling from his neck, greeted us with a smile. Spotting Liam, he stood up and took his hands, "What a delightful surprise. And who is this with you?"

Liam introduced me as a friend from France. The Bishop asked me about my experiences in Aix and how I met Liam. When I told him about the Internet dating site, the Bishop opened his eyes wide and looked at me and then scowled at Liam. Liam quickly excused himself to use the rest room.

When he left, the Bishop walked close to me. He took my hands into his, gazed directly into my eyes, and said, "My child" —even though I was older than he was—"be very careful with whom you keep company."

Whatever does he mean? Before I could ask him, Liam reentered the room.

I nodded my head and said, "I will, thank you."

Liam announced that it was time to leave. He never asked what the Bishop said, and I didn't volunteer the information.

We hopped back on the Hop-On, Hop-Off bus and returned to our hotel.

That night, we each slept in our own bed. Liam took what I presumed was a preparatory shower for romance. This was only date two, after all! Being a sound sleeper, I fell asleep still pondering the statement of the Bishop.

The next morning, Liam and I went to the National Gallery. The walk for him was difficult from the bus stop. I liked this man, but with my energy, I was not sure we made a good fit.

When we reached the Gallery, he chose to wait for me in the café instead of viewing the world-famous art. Then I *knew* we were not a fit. I enjoyed the paintings and sculptures for several hours before returning to pick up my companion. He had spent the time with Guinness and shots of Jameson. I had heard that the Irish were drinkers. Liam fit the stereotype.

Dinner that evening was at a charming little bistro in our hotel neighborhood, so unremarkable and tiny we almost passed it with its dark windows.

Inside, antiques filled the small foyer. We were told they had no open tables for the two of us, but we could sit at the community table. The food at the restaurant had been highly recommended by the concierge, so we agreed to stay. We were led into the main dining room filled with classic furniture. Farm implements hung on the walls. Lanterns with candles on the tables illuminated the room, giving it a romantic atmosphere. Our hostess led us to a table large enough for eight.

One other person was sitting there, a slightly overweight, middle-aged man with gray hair. He asked, "Where are you from?"

When Liam revealed that he was from Newtown, Ireland, the other diner grew excited.

He gave Liam a hearty handshake. "My name is Dan. I lived there for many years and still have relatives in Newtown. I now live in New York. I'm here on business."

Liam and Dan had much in common and spent most of the dinner talking about Newtown and people they knew, leaving me to listen and interject thoughts from time to time. So much for a romantic meal!

Dan left the restaurant before we did, though not before paying for our wine out of gratitude for the camaraderie. A nice gesture.

Feeling the glow from the alcohol, Liam and I walked arm in arm on the way back to the hotel. A pleasant, relaxed emotion flowed between us on our third date.

Back in our hotel room, Liam moved to give me a passionate kiss. I stepped closer. He embraced me. I nestled into his shoulder. At last!

"Ouch," cried Liam

I stepped back. "What's wrong?"

He recoiled. "My shoulder," he shouted. "I have an arthritic shoulder." He grabbed his upper arm and lay down on the bed — without me.

"I just need time to work it out."

I stood there with my mouth wide open. The moment which started out so promisingly had passed.

I now dubbed him My Boozing Little Leprechaun with a bum shoulder!

The next morning I repacked my blue satin nightgown, still in its beautifully wrapped tissue, wondering if it would ever make an appearance.

After Liam dressed, I asked, "How's the shoulder?"

"Glory be, much better." He gazed into my eyes. "Ah, I love ye now, Ca- rinn, I want to meet again, soon."

"You are a dear man," I said. *But* not *in my lifetime!*

My experience was typical of Internet dating. A person often seemed so interesting while emailing and Skyping, but it wasn't until spending time together that the chemistry revealed itself — or not. I wanted the match to work and perhaps overlooked cues I should have picked up while still in the Skype stage.

Liam and I have not seen one another again, but we Skype from time to time. I needed someone to be a companion, who appreciated art, was spiritual, and cared for me. As dear as My Little Leprechaun was, his preference for Guinness and Jameson left us little time for mutual interests. Spending time with him made me realize what I needed in a man.

I wondered why I couldn't find romance in France, of all places. Would I ever find another soul mate like Bill?

On later reflection, I realized I looked for love on the outside, but my shattered hopes pulled me deeper inside to ponder:

What lesson did I really need to learn?

Shepherd's Pie

Ingredients

1 tablespoon vegetable oil

1 large onion, peeled and chopped

1 large carrot, peeled and chopped

1 pound ground lamb (or other ground meat)

1 cup beef or chicken broth

1 tablespoon tomato paste

1 teaspoon chopped fresh or dry rosemary

1 tablespoon chopped fresh Italian parsley

1 cup frozen peas

2 pounds russet potatoes, peeled and cut into chunks

6 tablespoons unsalted butter

1/2 cup milk

salt to taste

Preheat oven to 375°F (190°C).

In a large sauté pan over medium-high heat, heat the oil, then add the onion, carrots, and meat. Cook until browned, 8 to 10 minutes.

Drain the fat and add the broth, tomato paste, and herbs. Simmer until the juices thicken, about 10 minutes, then add the peas.

Pour the mixture into a 1 1/2-quart baking dish; set aside.

Meanwhile, bring the potatoes to a boil in salted water. Cook until tender, about 20 minutes; drain.

Mash the potatoes with the butter, milk, and salt.

Spread them over the meat mixture, then crosshatch the top with a fork.

Bake until golden, 30 to 35 minutes.

Makes 6 servings.

CHAPTER 15

The Dark Night of the Soul

The Gifts That Come From Darkness

Weeks after my visit with Liam, I pondered my relationships with Floyd, Jan, and Liam. I was shocked at my own apparent neediness to be with a man. What was this all about?

Because I was friendly and outgoing, I believed I would become involved in a relationship easily. But connecting with anyone other than Mark, who had moved back to England, had not happened. I wondered why. I had met many men. Was it because I had announced that I would only be here for a year? Was it because I did not speak the language? Never did I imagine it had to do with my age. My spirit and *joie de vivre* always trumped age in my mind. Besides, I had been gifted with genes that made me appear and have the energy of a woman fifteen years my junior.

I had lots of love to give to the right person. And I didn't feel too old. Ever so slowly, I imagined that my age had something to do with my lack of a relationship. Did everyone eventually reach the end of his or her sexual attractiveness? Had I reached mine?

As I brushed my hair in the bedroom, I looked into the ornate mirror on the wall. I really looked at my face without my usual jovial self. What I saw shocked me — a sober face with wrinkles around my eyes and lines on my chin. When had they appeared? Is this what others saw when they looked at me? Not the adventurous, fun-loving, spirited person I thought myself to be?

My first realization was that I had somehow believed what I had been told by society — that a woman, in particular, was only attractive if she was young, thin, and stylish. This not too subtle message was conveyed on every advertisement for selling clothes, cars, and liquor. That concept plagued me because I was no longer young and had put on weight since arriving in France. Holding on to that old idea of what was attractive created darkness and a downhill spiral. If I let it go, the void would lead to sadness, as loss does. And I had no concept of what would replace the old belief. I seemed to be going around in circles in my mind.

However, I saw women who didn't fit society's norm of attractiveness finding a mate. How did they do it? What was their mate-worthy secret? I had much to learn from them in the area of attractiveness.

I made a list of what I admired in men and found attractive. They were: open to new ideas; honest; intelligent; healthy; interested in physical fitness; curious; positive; interested in personal and spiritual growth;

fun and humorous; adventurous; and loved traveling. Just like me!

I imagined a man would have a similar list of qualities he looked for in a woman. I noticed that I didn't list any physical attributes, but I wondered if men put youth, beauty, and sexiness at the top of their list.

Perhaps physical attributes were not the only means of allure. My list suggested that common interests could bring two people together. Had I not been sharing who I was to generate an interest in this foreign country? Had I been too busy learning from others that I gave less of myself?

This threw me into further soul-searching. I gazed at my reflection in the mirror. Did I have anything of interest to say? I was well versed in counseling and caretaking of a husband. I could easily talk about those topics, but neither suggested common interests with a Frenchman, unless he needed counseling or caretaking. I remembered the Frenchwomen who all conversed in depth about a variety of topics. Many knew their country's history and talked about political issues.

Still searching my soul, I questioned myself. But what I was not aware of at the time were the challenges inherent in moving to a foreign country. Challenges became more difficult when living alone. Especially when loneliness set in. My eagerness to fulfill my long-held dream to live in France kept me in denial about this. I thought of Ivan Ilyich in *The Death of Ivan Ilyich* by Leo Tolstoy and his regrets on his deathbed. He said, "What if my whole life had been wrong?" I didn't want the regret of not fulfilling my dream of living in France.

Mountain Sainte Victoire from Cezanne's painting place

I gazed in the mirror. "What would you, Karin, do if you could no longer be in a love relationship? What would fill your life? Would you have a purpose?" *Oh, to not have a lover or a purpose. What a huge loss.*

My former goal of becoming an Aixoise by learning the culture and touring surrounding villages seemed frivolous now, a nice sideline but not really worthy enough to be my life's purpose. I reviewed my life's purpose. Before coming to Aix, I had considered writing a book. It would encapsulate my life lessons that I often shared with my counseling clients. Sometimes a client would understand a concept more clearly if I told a personal story. I thought again about that book, I decided it fell flat and I lost interest in writing it. But writing about my discoveries in Aix felt new and fresh. Writing a book would inspire others to fulfill their dreams. I had moved from my old purpose to a new one.

I faced the mirror again and gave myself a good talking to. "Writing your book may be your life's purpose, but writing about Bill and his illness must be postponed until later. Get out of the apartment and into this beautiful spring day. Write and have fun!"

The reflection winked, "Yes."

The break I needed was a walk in the countryside. I looked to the sunny day to bring light to my dark mood. But before I set out, I tucked some chocolate brownies into my purse — for nourishment. I decided to venture to Cezanne's painting place in Aix, where he had the view of the Sainte-Victoire mountain. He painted it more than one hundred times. He frequently packed his painting equipment and walked the ten minutes from his studio.

I hadn't been there yet, and it was only a twenty-minute stroll.

The City of Aix revered Cezanne so much that they made this place a landmark. The area was lined with stepping-stones from the street up to the spot where he painted, which provided a view to his beloved mountain. Here, also, were weatherproof copies of many of his paintings displayed outdoors, all labeled with the whereabouts of the original painting.

As I stood in awe on the very spot the famous artist set up his easel to create, I tried to see what he saw those many years ago. Sainte-Victoire in the distance showed its familiar sharp, limestone peak. While I enjoyed the area for many minutes, the sun changed the shadows on the mountainside, revealing why he painted so many pictures with different results. I shared a similar fascination with Cezanne, that illumination altered perception. We both knew that light changed the mountain, just as I knew that light on my darkened soul would reveal answers to my questions. I took consolation in knowing we all have mountains in life that change when we "see the light." I snapped photos and felt inspired to write, but realized there was nowhere to sit. I continued up the road to find another quiet spot.

Soon, I came to a musty-smelling stone bridge in the shade of a plane tree. I sat down and wrote about my trip to Amsterdam, feeling gratitude for no longer thinking of the demise of Bill.

A car stopped. A man rolled down his window and asked a question in French. I caught a few words and made it obvious I didn't understand.

"*Parlez-vous Anglais?*" I asked.

With that, a fifty-something-year-old man stepped out of his Fiat. He was nice looking, with blue eyes and blond hair, and a little overweight.

"Do you know where Cezanne's Atelier is located?" he asked.

I gave him directions, then informed him about the painting area where I had just been. He told me he had arrived from Belgium for a wedding and was staying with his uncle who lived up the road.

"Do you know the Granet Museum with many impressionist paintings in *centre ville*?" I asked.

"Yes, I'm going there after the Atelier and then to lunch..." He paused as if to extend an invitation.

I thought he seemed a nice person, and lonesome. He lived in Belgium and would be here for only four days. *Don't get involved.* That thought made me realize how depressed I was. I didn't even feel inclined to extend myself for a nice afternoon, and who knew what else. I laughed at myself. I'm not like Floyd who collects people from all over the world.

Deep in thought, I watched Mr. No Name get back into his car and drive away. I was relieved, but also concerned at my apathy.

The next day, I was on the phone telling my friend, Marie Paule, the story of the man from Belgium and my reluctance to get involved.

"That doesn't sound like you, Karin. You are always up for an adventure," came her observation.

Another day, in town I caught my reflection in a shop window. I was shocked to see that my usually blonde hair had turned dark and was in desperate need of a haircut. With that awareness, I made immediate plans for a cut and a lighter color. My depression caused me to ignore my appearance, I still knew that looking better on the outside would affect my mood. So I made an appointment with the hairdresser as an act of love. Since self-love was on the agenda, I dived into my purse to retrieve a dark brownie. Dark chocolate was my mood enhancer.

My enthusiasm for my year of discovery had kept me from confronting my aging. Maybe I was too old to attract a man on looks alone. Yet age had nothing to do with my inward journey. I realized I had moved from a lifelong feeling of not being enough to being good enough. That resulted in giving myself permission to reflect and write. I would pour my love into writing a book, not only to inspire others, but to express self-love.

The Blue Satin Nightgown was lovingly conceived from that revelation.

Mood Enhancing Dark Chocolate Brownies

Ingredients

1/2 cup white sugar

2 tablespoons butter

2 tablespoons water

1 1/2 cups semisweet chocolate chips

2 eggs

1/2 teaspoon vanilla extract

2/3 cup all-purpose flour

1/4 teaspoon baking soda

1/2 teaspoon salt

Preheat the oven to 325°F (165°C). Grease an 8x8-inch square pan.

In a medium saucepan, combine the sugar, butter, and water. Cook over medium heat until boiling. Remove from heat and stir in chocolate chips until melted and smooth. Mix in the eggs and vanilla. Combine the flour, baking soda, and salt; stir into the chocolate mixture. Spread evenly into the prepared pan.

Bake for 25 to 30 minutes in the preheated oven, until brownies set up. Do not overbake! Cool in pan and cut into squares.

Consume a brownie whenever you need to treat yourself.

My movers around my table

CHAPTER 16

A New Door Opens

I Can Make a Home Anywhere I Roam

On Saturday morning, I sat at a long table in the back room at Croquemitoufle. A group of expats and French met at the little restaurant two mornings a week for coffee and conversation. Nicole, a Frenchwoman with dyed brilliant red hair, and I were in conversation when I noticed Robert sitting across from me. Nicole, a friend of his, whispered to me, "He is seventy years old, and never been married. You would have to stand in line if you had any intentions of changing that status."

I didn't tell her, but I had no desire to become involved with Robert, or any other man, after my earlier misadventures with Mark, Floyd, Jan, and Liam.

I ordered *un café avec un tarte tatin* (apple tart), then shared with Nicole, "I don't know what I'm going to do about my apartment. It has only two small windows and is very dark. The disco below me plays loud music every Friday and Saturday nights. It's impossible to sleep until 1 or 2 a.m., especially with the *ba boom, ba boom* beat of the disco. I want to write in a quiet place filled with light."

"Furnished apartments are hard to find in the *centre ville*," said Nicole. "Maybe Robert can help."

She tapped Robert on his arm and told him about my problem.

He beamed. "I have a furnished one that is available. Not in the *centre ville*, and it only has one bedroom, but you may look at it if you like."

Yippee, a chance to get some regular sleep, I thought to myself.

The tall, thin, Frenchman was a regular attendee and well respected by all who knew him. I discovered later that Robert had very limited vision due to a progressive eye disease. That forced him to retire early from being a pharmacist. However, he still owned a pharmacy store in north Aix en Provence.

I overheard him talk to iPhone's Siri to contact Anne, his sister. After a brief phone chat, he said to me, "My sister can drive us to the flat tomorrow."

My enthusiasm for the possibility of a new place was diminished when Nicole told me later that his apartment was dark and the furniture heavy and old. However, imagining living with peace and quiet where I could reflect and write made me eager to see the place.

The next day, Anne, driving a typically small French car, picked me up. I greeted her and Robert, then climbed into the back seat, my knees under my chin.

Robert's flat was not in the *centre ville*, as he had said, but rather quite a way up a hill. This dampened my spirits, but he assured me I could either walk or take one of two buses to get to and from town. I wasn't so keen on taking buses.

We soon arrived at the gated complex, which Anne told me was a former farm. That accounted for the spacious grounds with many mature trees and flowerbeds around the parking area. Anne told me there were five large buildings, each containing three floors with two flats each.

We climbed to the second level. Anne unlocked the door and invited me in. I took a deep breath, anticipating a better home.

What first came into view was the lightness of the rooms, due to two sliding glass walls that stretched the entire width of the living and dining rooms. The doors led to a wide terrace. It overlooked the park-like grounds of the property. On the other side of the unit, the kitchen and bedroom area featured large windows with another view of trees and flowerbeds. Spectacular!

I surveyed the furniture. Yes, it was dated, but in fact, most of the large hand-carved pieces were antiques. In fact, an elegant desk faced the terrace and garden. A perfect spot for writing. Magnificent! To lift my spirits, there were cheerful, original artworks on the walls, all hung at eye level for six-foot Robert. An easy fix for my five-foot frame.

"I love your place. How soon can I move in?"

"It is available now," Robert replied. "I just need the first month's rent."

I was thinking of how different this was from renting my first place. Then, I was required to pay the first month's rent, a security deposit equal to a month's rent, a finder's fee for the *immoblier*, and a renter's insurance policy for one year.

I announced at the next Croquemitoufle meeting that I found a new apartment and needed some help with the move. Within five minutes, two men and two women volunteered. One woman packed my belongings, another unpacked, one man drove his car, and the other loaded the boxes. My move magically came together as I occupied my new home.

I celebrated their help and friendship with a luncheon I prepared in my new kitchen. I spread a white lace tablecloth on the round dining room table from which we ate, drank bottles of rosé wine, and talked for five hours!

For months, I luxuriated in the peace and quiet of this garden setting. From the terrace, I watched the birds in the trees and the critters who lived below. The two most prevalent black and white birds were magpies. I remembered my mother telling me of her experience when she was a little girl of the magpies in Utah stealing anything shiny and hiding it in their favorite hiding spot. With that idea in mind, I put several pieces of aluminum foil along the railing of the terrace and waited for them to disappear. I wanted to befriend the birds. I had high hopes of even taming and training these creatures. After a few days, I was disappointed to notice the foil remained there, so I changed to small pieces of leftover baguette. These, too, were untouched. Even so, magpies kept me company while I wrote about my adventures.

I went through the seasons in that lovely apartment. I witnessed the changing scenes from the terrace. First came the flowering chestnut trees with their lacy, tall, Christmas tree-shaped blossoms. Later, the trees next to the terrace filled with blazing rosy-pink blossoms. As the color faded, leaves began to appear on the trees, transforming my view into a park-like setting. On the ground, the beds came alive with yellow daffodils followed by purple irises. In the summer, the aromatic lavender, so famous in Provence, sent their fragrance wafting up to my terrace.

And as Robert predicted, I formed a pattern when going to and from town. I walked down the hill past many apartment buildings, crossing the main road, the *périphérique*, down the narrow Avenue Sapporo, dodging the traffic with the other pedestrians, past Cathédrale St-Sauveur and into the *centre ville*. However, climbing back up the hill took me many months to brave, so in the meantime I hopped on the number seven or ten bus to my stop, Les Muriers Blancs.

Typing away during those months in Robert's apartment, I learned a valuable lesson. When you make a decision to follow your dreams, the Universe will support you. The Universe gifted me with the perfect quiet spot to write and make my home in this foreign land.

Tarte Tatin
Apple Tart

This is a very traditional French dessert and worth the effort.

Ingredients

1 10 1/2 inch tart shell

5 pounds tart apples such as Pippin, peeled, halved, and cored

1 1/2 cups sugar

10 tablespoons butter, cut in thin slices

Line a round baking sheet with parchment paper or lightly flour it.

Roll out the pastry on a lightly floured work surface to form an 11-inch round. Transfer the pastry to the prepared baking sheet and refrigerate for at least 1 hour.

Spread the sugar evenly over the bottom of a very heavy 10 1/2 -inch ovenproof skillet or flameproof baking pan. Place the butter slices evenly over the sugar, then arrange the apple halves on top of the butter. Begin at the outside edge and stand the halves on their sides, facing in one direction with stem ends toward the center. Pack the apples as close together as possible, gently pushing them together so they are held standing by pressure. Make a second circle of apple halves inside the first, packing them in on their edges as well. Place one apple half right in the center of the second circle to fill in the small space that remains. The idea is to get as many apples into the pan as possible, while keeping them nicely arranged.

Place the skillet over medium-low heat and cook the apples in the butter and sugar, uncovered, until the sugar turns golden brown; this will take at least 1 hour. Watch the apples closely to be sure they don't stick; you may want to adjust the heat now and then, to slow down or speed up the cooking. As the sugar and butter melt and the apples give up some of their juices, baste the apples occasionally with a turkey baster. Gradually, the sugar will caramelize the apples nearly all the way through, though they will remain uncooked on top.

Preheat the oven to 425°F (218°C).

When the cooking juices are deep golden and the apples are nearly cooked through, remove the pastry from the refrigerator and quickly and carefully place it over the apples, gently pushing it down around them, simultaneously easing it toward the center so that if it shrinks on the sides there will still be enough of it to cover the apples. Using a sharp knife, trim off and discard any extra pastry.

Place the skillet on a baking sheet. Bake in the center of the oven until the pastry is golden, 25 to 30 minutes.

Remove the skillet from the oven. Immediately invert a serving platter with a slight lip over the skillet. Quickly invert so the crust is on the bottom. Remove the skillet. Should any apples stick to it, gently remove them and reinsert them into their rightful place in the tart.

Serve generous slices as soon as the tart has cooled slightly, but is still very warm.

Entrance to Cezanne's studio

CHAPTER 17

The Unknown American Hero

Don't Wait to Express Appreciation

I began each day with a familiar ritual. Stepping to the elegantly carved wooden desk by the terrace window, I set down my glass of water, tuned to the Chris Botti radio station for some soothing music, and looked out the sunny windows to check on my familiar magpies. Today they hadn't taken the pieces of baguette, but were hovering around to keep me company.

I sat down and prepared to write. That always took me deeper into myself. Today was no exception. I reflected on my life and how many changes had come about since that day when I decided to act on my dream and move to France. Not only the outward changes of meeting and visiting interesting places I'd been, but also the intangible shifts. I finally confronted my age, and I saw that I was enough. The big one I recognized; that as my heart opened, I had love for myself. I felt more alive and saw events happening around me that had previously gone unnoticed. I valued everyday events with new respect and wanted to celebrate small interactions by marking and talking to participants. I wanted to interact with the world and be counted as part of the living.

I recalled one particular event that stood out when I went about my errands in *centre ville*. I entered my favorite frame shop to have three prints of water scenes by Monet and Cezanne featured at the Granet Museum Exhibition matted and framed. I spotted a customer. The man stood quietly, waiting while the clerk finished up with a customer. He was of medium height, black hair, with a heavy black mustache. His dark brown eyes revealed a tension, and yet he stood perfectly at attention, holding a Federal Express envelope.

I caught his eyes and said, "*Bonjour.*" He nodded his head, but said nothing.

When the clerk waited on him, he stoically opened up his envelope and spoke in English. "I want to have these put into a shadow box frame. Can you help me?" He carefully took four small boxes out of the envelope.

He went on to say, "I just retired from forty years in the American Army. My daughter insists I have these framed."

My curiosity got the best of me. "Excuse me, but you say you had just retired from forty years of service?"

"Yes, ma'am," came his clipped reply.

I felt the urge to connect. The new me couldn't resist asking, "Pardon me. May I see what you have in those boxes?"

"Certainly." He handed them to me. Jagged, deep scars marked his upper left arm.

The clear plastic covers on the boxes revealed two American Purple Hearts and two medals I couldn't identify. I held the boxes as if I was holding something sacred. "When did you receive these?"

"The first in 1980 and the second in 1988."

"I am sorry, but what are the other medals?"

"The Distinguished Medals of Honor, one gold and one silver."

"How did you earn those?"

He merely said, "Over and above the call of duty."

All I could do was shake my head in awe. Tears began to well up in my eyes. I cleared my throat, and finally got out the words, "Where were you when you earned these distinguished awards?"

Again he so humbly and simply said, "One for duty in Iraq and the other from Afghanistan."

Tears trickled down my face. I said quietly, "Thank you for making the world a safer place. I appreciate your strength and courage and admire you."

I was hoping that he felt my gratitude as I handed him back the four small boxes that represented so much sacrifice.

I thought of Bill and my three brothers who had served in the military. Bill was in the Navy, two brothers were in the Air Force, and the third served in the Merchant Marines. My brothers never talked about their experiences, while Bill always joked that he fought the battle of Corpus Christi, Texas. All four were now dead. I never thanked them for what they had done.

I continued to admire this unknown hero as he talked to the clerk about the mounting of his treasures. I wanted to invite him out to coffee to learn more about him and his accomplishments, but thought it would be unfair to ask anymore from a man who had given so much.

That night, it came to me. I should have hosted a party to honor him and his family for his years of service. Unfortunately, the moment had passed. I had no way to contact him. I had lost an opportunity to know him better, just as I had lost that time with Bill and my brothers as well.

All I could hope for was that he recognized my tears as an expression of immense gratitude.

I typed on my computer, "Don't wait to express appreciation. You may not get another chance."

Chicken and Dumplings

The comfort food I wished I had prepared for that Unknown American Hero and his family.

Broth

Ingredients

1 whole chicken

2 tablespoons olive oil

1 yellow onion, chopped

1 stalk of celery, sliced

6 carrots, sliced

2 bay leaves

pinch *herbes de Provence*

Salt/pepper

Dumplings

Ingredients

1 cup flour

2 teaspoons baking powder

1/2 teaspoon salt

1 egg

Milk

Directions for broth

Heat olive oil in a large stockpot. Cook onion, celery, and carrots until limp. Add chicken and cover with water. Add bay leaves, *herbes de Provence*, salt and pepper. Bring water to a boil, cover, and simmer for a minimum of 2 hours, adding water as it evaporates to keep chicken covered.

After cooking for 2 hours, remove chicken to a bowl and strain broth and vegetables in a colander. Return broth to stockpot and continue simmering to reduce to become more flavorful.

When chicken is cool enough to handle, remove meat, discarding skin and bones. Cut meat into small pieces and return to broth.

Add whatever vegetables desired in soup, such as new potatoes, carrots, and peas. Cook until tender.

Directions for dumplings

Mix flour, baking powder, and salt in a bowl. Break egg into a measuring cup. Add enough milk to measure 1/2 cup. Beat well and add slowly to the dry ingredients. Drop by tablespoons into boiling broth. Lower heat so that broth simmers. Cook covered for 5 minutes. Uncover and cook for another 5 minutes.

Serve immediately to four hungry eaters.

CHAPTER 18

My French Makeover Goes To California

When you are inspired by some extraordinary project, all your thoughts break their bonds: your mind transcends limitations; your consciousness expands in every direction; and you find yourself in a new, great wonderful world.

Patañjali

In mid-September, Marie Paule and I sat outside in the late afternoon at the legendary Brasserie Deux Garçons on Cours Mirabeau, enjoying a glass of rosé. I admired the plane trees with their leaves turning yellow and dying.

"You know, Marie Paule, I will be leaving for California soon."

Tears welled in her brown eyes. "I don't want to think about it." My petite, fifty-year-old friend with her beautifully coiffed hair pulled out a hanky. She wiped her eyes.

I reached for her arm to comfort her. "I don't like thinking of it either, but I have family who are expecting me. I miss them."

She sniffed, "Have the past two years been a good time for you, being so far away from home?"

"Oh, yes, more than I expected. I had planned to be here for a year, but it was so wonderful I stayed for two. Seeing so many villages, making new friends, and traveling with visiting family. Remember when I came to your cooking class? I was so timid about speaking French. I'm so glad we became good friends. I so cherish you and your husband Xavier."

"*Oui, bonne amie.*"

"You're a good friend. You did so much for me — taking me shopping, translating at government offices, teaching me French cooking. I hope I mean as much to you."

She squeezed my arm. "You have become part of my life."

"Your friendship has made it even more wonderful. When I first arrived, all I could think of were the adventures I'd be having and becoming a part of Provence on my own. Having my favorite *boulangerie*, shopping the *marché*, and cooking local food. I wanted to explore surrounding villages and get to know them as well. I didn't think much beyond that. I just wanted to become *Aixoise*. Aix has become my muse, a beautiful place to live while I learned about the culture and myself." I took another sip of wine and pondered a moment. "You made me realize my true purpose. Previously, my purpose had been counseling clients, raising my children, and my husband, and caring for him when he was gravely ill. You stood by me as I discovered a new life. Now I want to inspire other seniors to live an extraordinary life. I'm like Don Quixote battling windmills with my big ideas about life!" I said, mocking my ambitions.

"Don't be so hard on yourself," she said. "In retirement, you should know you've earned the right to enjoy life."

"I'm just not a person who can sit around doing nothing. I need to have meaning in my life."

"My mother is like that. She takes care of my father and is available for my daughter. That is her life's purpose." Marie Paule looked at her watch. "Speaking of family, I must get home to prepare dinner for them. That is my purpose today."

We finished our wine and hugged goodbye, followed by two big *bisous* on each cheek. We bid each other *au revoir* and headed in different directions.

On my way home, I saw all the places I would miss, like the *marché* where I bought seasonal produce fresh from the farm. I loved the hustle and bustle of the shoppers. I strolled through the flower market and smelled the fragrance of the blooms. I wandered past Jean Biguine Coiffures and waved to my hairdresser Alexandre. How would I replace him and a French cut?

I continued strolling up the hill, realizing I had lived without a car for two years. What an unthinkable idea in California. My life had slowed down. Who had time to hang clothes to dry or to wash dishes by hand in Orange

County? I wanted to bring this slower French pace back to the United States. I wanted to hold onto how the French cherished interactions with people and made time for them. I remembered the first luncheon I hosted where I sat with new friends around the dining table for five hours, just talking about everything and anything. There was no request for the TV to watch the news or a football game. No one brought out cell phones to check for emails.

I gave myself credit for being open to making mistakes about language, customs, and etiquette. I chuckled about the time I used the word *Aixois*, a male living in Aix, when referring to myself, instead of *Aixoise*, a female living in Aix.

I sat on my terrace looking at the garden below. The cicadas grew silent for the day as the evening glow softened the view of the dying sunflowers. I looked around the apartment that had been my cozy home in Aix. Would I miss it when I returned to California? Would I pine for all that Aix had come to mean? I spied a tea towel decorated with one of Toulouse Lautrec's paintings. Bill had picked it out in Paris. With that, my mind flashed to the joy I felt here with the spirit of my Francophile Bill still with me, enhancing my life.

The makeover that began as a result of scattering Bill's ashes in Paris now felt complete. What began as an adventure in discovery of the French culture turned into a discovery of self. Yes, my dream of living in France had been fulfilled and the makeover completed.

Just as Hemingway knew in *A Moveable Feast* that experiences become a part of you and never leave you, I, too, knew my time in France had changed me. I would take what I learned with me wherever I went. I could create a life for myself anywhere, and I could attract like-minded spirits to my outgoing nature and humor. I didn't know what my next exciting discovery would be, but I knew when I left Aix, my experiences here would remain with me the rest of my life.

I moved back to California in September, 2014. My planned one year in France had turned into two. Clearly, one year had not been enough. I returned with new eyes. It didn't matter that the blue satin nightgown was still wrapped in its tissue.

Back in my home state, I found a beach cottage in my beloved Laguna Beach, a town that resonated with my heart. The village attracted artists and creative people. Sculptures crafted by local artisans dotted the village. There was an open-minded spirit with a range of activities that brought people together in community.

My friends, and even strangers, were impressed with my French adventure. They would ask, "What did you learn while in France?" At first, I told them about the language, the culture, and the cooking classes. Then I revealed more. "My experience taught me that I am enough, that I need not measure my worth against others."

By following my dream to do the unthinkable of moving to a foreign country where I knew no one and didn't speak the language, I gained a confidence my seventy-eight years in the United States hadn't given me. As I settled into my beach community, I renewed old friendships and incorporated my French lifestyle while completing *The Blue Satin Nightgown.*

Instead of my previous hectic pace, I adopted the mindful chore of washing my dishes, foregoing the convenience of a dishwasher. I spent time having conversations with my family and friends, without thinking of the endless "to do" lists. I even maintained my French way of dressing and avoided the showy, glitzy new styles so prevalent on TV and in American magazines. Provence taught me to savor the freshness of food from the *marché*, so I relished shopping for foods at the Laguna Beach Farmer's Market.

I have been home for a year, time enough to reflect on revelations that came from writing *The Blue Satin Nightgown.* That nightgown had quite a journey from France to Amsterdam, back to France, and then onto London, ever hopeful of finding romance. In the end, it stayed in the pristine wrapped tissue from the lingerie boutique, teaching me I had been looking in the wrong place.

During my travels, I discovered I was really searching for a love partner, someone who was precious. Finally, it dawned on me. I must love myself first and foremost. That was my French makeover. It was time to unwrap the Blue Satin Nightgown and wear it for myself!

Ooh la la!

Just as I provided recipes after each chapter, I end with my final concoction gleaned from revelations revealed during my makeover. I hope they add spice to your life:

1. Age is not a limitation. Live your dream whether you are twenty or eighty.
2. Discomfort is part of learning. Endure discomfort to reap the rewards of learning and enriching your life.
3. See the world with new eyes. Or as Henry Thoreau said, "It's not what you look at that matters, it's what you see." Discover something new every day, as if you are living in a foreign country where everything is unfamiliar.
4. Life with all of its adventures is a "Moveable Feast." Take risks and create adventures.
5. Life is sweeter with family, friends, and a mate. Make time to enjoy them.
6. Do not depend on the superficiality of physical appearance. Redefine attractiveness and love your essence.
7. Bliss may be right in front of you. Be open to romancing your life with beauty.
8. Don't wait for the opportunity to express appreciation. Tell others what you appreciate about them now.
9. Don't take all that you have for granted. Practice gratitude.
10. Love will bring you a sense of wellbeing and contentment. Recognize how many people love you. But most importantly, love yourself just as you are.

Entrance to Beautiful Place Hotel de Ville

I hope you enjoyed my recipes to feed your body and nourish your soul. My goal was to inspire you to live your dream, regardless of your age. If I could live in a foreign country without knowing anyone or the language, you too can begin a whole new adventure.

One word of caution: when you take the step to live your dream, you will enrich your life in ways you could never imagine. You will come alive, love yourself, and bring that spirit to the world.

Do the unthinkable. Follow your dreams and have a makeover. And what the heck, wear a Blue Satin Nightgown!

LOVE AFTER LOVE

The time will come
when, with elation
you will greet yourself arriving
at your own door, in your own mirror
and each will smile at the other's welcome,

and say, sit here. Eat.
You will love again the stranger who was your self.
Give wine. Give bread. Give back your heart
to itself, to the stranger who has loved you

all your life, whom you ignored
for another, who knows you by heart.
Take down the love letters from the bookshelf,

the photographs, the desperate notes,
peel your own image from the mirror.
Sit. Feast on your life.

Derek Walcott

Acknowledgments

I am grateful to Wendy Rohm, my first writing instructor and the one who loved the concept of my book and knew there would be an enormous readership among those needing a little push to live their dream. Thank you for all of your miraculous editing and your faith.

To Leonard Szymczak, a great big hug for never giving up on me. Your wisdom as shown through encouragement, editing, and sense of humor has made working with you a joy.

To Claire McAlpine, I will always have gratitude for your faith in my writing and the suggestions you made along the way. You were the one who suggested and helped me enter "The Good Life France" writing competition 2014 and win!

I will always be grateful to Diana Wentworth for your inspiring Foreword and support throughout my writing process.

To Judy Wright, who believed in my writing from the very beginning and helped with many rewrites.

To Rosemary Daniell, who was the one who told me I must reveal my age, a huge thank you. It took courage, but you were right!

Thank you, *Les Plumes* writing group in Aix-en-Provence and our indomitable leader Susan Stone.

Thank you, Mary Harris, Fiona Jayde, and Tamara Cribley for treating my "baby" with the care and efficiency you would treat your own. You have my appreciation.

I am grateful to the following people for their careful and insightful reading of earlier drafts of this book: Nicia Anderson, Karen Tyner, Anita Hayward, Bud Morris, Paul McNeese, Joanne Tathum, and Mike Hammond. Your many suggestions have a home in *The Blue Satin Nightgown*.

To Edourd Halin, who so generously corrected my French language between shifts at LuLu's Creperie.

I am grateful for the ongoing support I have received from the members of Inside Edge and Inspirit Center for Spiritual Living, especially Ronn Sarno and June Crockett, for helping me with my book launch party.

I am also grateful to my book club members who always ask how the book is coming along: Lynette LaRoche, Peggy Anatol, Pat Carels, Annette Pattison, Roz Hoover, Geri Taylor, Anita Hayward, and Judy Wright.

To my two beautiful daughters, Wendy Bayley and Vicki Jett, for their ongoing encouragement and support of my endeavors.

About Karin Crilly, MFC

Karin Crilly is a retired Marriage and Family Counselor. She spent thirty satisfying years in private practice in Southern California. Her specialties were grief issues, esteem issues, and working with children utilizing Play Therapy. These areas arose from her background in teaching Special Education at the elementary school level and experiencing the loss of her own two husbands.

Born in Los Angeles, California, she grew up in Ojai, California and currently lives in Laguna Beach, California after having two adventurous years living in Aix-en-Provence, France.

In addition to teaching in the Ojai Unified School District and counseling in private practice, she served as Director of Counseling at Blind Children's Learning Center in Tustin, California supporting grieving parents, teaching numerous parenting classes, and supervising MFC Interns from CSUF and CSULB.

Her education includes two Master of Arts degrees, one in Marriage and Family Therapy and the other in Special Education from California Lutheran University located in Thousand Oaks California. Crilly's undergraduate degree is from La Verne University located in La Verne, California.

The first chapter of *The Blue Satin Nightgown, Scattered Dreams*, won the Good Life France writers contest in 2014. The five judges stated that out of 105 entries, hers moved them to tears.

46014334R00125

Made in the USA
San Bernardino, CA
23 February 2017